American Approaches to
World Affairs

THE CREDIBILITY OF INSTITUTIONS, POLICIES AND LEADERSHIP
A Series funded by the Hewlett Foundation
Kenneth W. Thompson, *Series Editor*

I. Ideas and Approaches to Politics and Foreign Policy
  Volume 1: Moralism and Morality in Politics and Diplomacy
  Kenneth W. Thompson
  Volume 2: The American Approach to Foreign Policy: A Pragmatic Perspective
  Cecil V. Crabb, Jr.
  Volume 3: Functionalism and Interdependence
  John Eastby
  Volume 4: American Approaches to World Affairs
  I. L. Claude

II. Institutions and Public Attitudes
  Volume 5: The Media
  Kenneth W. Thompson (ed.)
  Volume 6: The Private Sector
  J. Wilson Newman
  Volume 7: The President and the Public: Rhetoric and National Leadership
  Kathy B. and Craig Allen Smith (eds.)
  Volume 8: The Plimpton Papers—Law and Diplomacy
  Mrs. Francis T.P. Plimpton
  Volume 9: Bureaucracy and Statesmanship
  Robert A. Strong

III. Consensus and Public Policy
  Volume 10: The Last European Peace Conference: Paris 1946—Conflict of Values
  Stephen Kertesz

  Volume 11: Foreign Policy and Domestic Consensus
  Richard Melanson and Kenneth W. Thompson (eds.)
  Volume 12: Consensus: Issues and Problems
  Michael Joseph Smith and Kenneth W. Thompson (eds.)
  Volume 13: McCarthyism and Consensus?
  William B. Ewald, Jr.
  Volume 14: Consensus and the American Mission
  Brian Klunk
  Volume 15: The United States Acquires the Philippines: Consensus vs. Reality
  Louis J. Halle

IV. Leaders and Credibility
  Volume 16: Essays on Leadership: Comparative Insights
  Kenneth W. Thompson (ed.)
  Volume 17: American Moral and Political Leadership in the Third World
  Kenneth W. Thompson (ed.)
  Volume 18: U.S. Leadership in Asia and the Middle East
  Kenneth W. Thompson (ed.)
  Volume 19: Winston S. Churchill: Philosopher and Statesman
  Michael Fowler
  Volume 20: Institutions and Leadership: Prospects for the Future
  Kenneth W. Thompson (ed.)

American Approaches to World Affairs

The Credibility of Institutions, Policies and Leadership
Volume 4

Inis L. Claude

Series Editor
Kenneth W. Thompson

University Press of America
Lanham • New York • London

Copyright © 1986 by

University Press of America,® Inc.

4720 Boston Way
Lanham, MD 20706

3 Henrietta Street
London WC2E 8LU England

All rights reserved
Printed in the United States of America

Library of Congress Cataloging in Publication Data

Claude, Inis, L.
  American approaches to world affairs.

  (The Credibility of institutions, policies, and
leadership ; v. 4)
  Bibliography: p.
  1. United States—Foreign relations— 1945—
  2. United States—Foreign relations administration.
  3. International relations.   I. Title.   II. Series.
  JX1417.C49   1986   327.73   86-1704
  ISBN 0-8191-5303-6 (alk. paper)
  ISBN 0-8191-5304-4 (pbk. : alk. paper)

The views expressed by the author(s) of this publication do not necessarily represent the opinions of the Miller Center. We hold to Jefferson's dictum that: "Truth is the proper and sufficient antagonist to error, and has nothing to fear from the conflict, unless, by human interposition, disarmed of her natural weapons, free argument and debate."

Co-published by arrangement with
The White Burkett Miller Center of Public Affairs,
University of Virginia

Contents

PREFACE
   Kenneth W. Thompson   *vii*
INTRODUCTION   *ix*

Part I   Continuity and Change in the American Approach to World Affairs   *3*

Part II   What to Do About Other People's Wars   *21*

Part III   The Rejection of Collective Security   *51*

PREFACE
Kenneth W. Thompson

A book of essays by Professor Inis L. Claude, Jr., is certain to be a work of lasting value. One can safely prophesy that this slender volume will be read by students and citizens for years to come. Especially for those of us who over the years have used his *Swords Into Plowshares* and *Power and International Relations*, his papers promise to be an occasion for genuine intellectual pleasure. Claude is a master craftsman both in his use of the English language and in his ability to grapple with complex social and political principles and issues.

Claude's book is the concluding one in a series of four on approaches to politics and international relations. The other three studies have considered moralism, pragmatism and interdependence. The fourth volume throws the net more broadly in encompassing such themes as Continuity and Change in the American Approach, What to Do About Other People's Wars and Collective Security. It considers some of the most fundamental questions of war and peace.

Because Claude has never been one to rest content with the perspectives of others, the hallmark of this volume is its originality. It brings fresh insights to old problems and new propositions to past controversies. Almost certainly, it will stimulate serious discussion and some debate. It is one of the studies that make a series on Institutions and Leadership a worthwhile endeavor.

INTRODUCTION

For about a century after the United States gained its independence, most Americans believed, most of the time, that what happened outside their country was not of vital importance to the United States. There were occasions, of course, when the impact of external events was strongly felt, but the routine life of Americans did not seem to be much affected by happenings abroad. During this period, the reverse was also true: the rest of the world was not fundamentally affected by the behavior of the United States. This country was a relatively minor and unimportant member of the states system dominated by the European powers, which may have had something to do with the fact that it was not often the object of external interference; not being threatening, the United States was not much threatened. The United States and the rest of the world were not preoccupied with each other.

In the second century of American independence, that situation has changed. Events elsewhere have come to have tremendous impact upon Americans, and, even though some vestige of the sense of being free to choose or reject involvement has been retained, the United States has developed the consciousness of being encompassed by, rather than isolated from, the world out there. That world, for its part, has come to take the United States seriously, and is profoundly interested in and affected by what the United States decides to do and not to do.

It may be that the world and the United States are a little afraid of each other; neither is altogether comfortable about its vulnerability to the other's clumsy and perhaps malevolent intrusions, and in truth neither is adept at understanding the other or at avoiding inadvertent violation of the other's sensitivities. The interdependence between the United States and the rest of the world produces ambivalent reactions on both sides.

On its side of the relationship, the United States fumbles to find the appropriate place for itself, somewhere in the zone bounded on the one side by its recognition that isolationism is no longer possible and on the other by its disillusionment with the life of a Great Power. American policy must try to manage both the world's effect upon the United States and the effect of the United States upon the world; the former task concerns the vital interests of the country, and the latter its most weighty responsibilities.

The essays that follow are intended as contributions to thinking about the handling of those dual tasks. They do not focus exclusively on the relationship between the United States and the rest of the world. Because other states also have such bilateral relationships with the world outside their boundaries, it is desirable to look generally at the question of how individual states deal with the larger system. Even though the case of every state is unique, we have much to learn from the experience of others.

The first essay is devoted to the argument that the American approach to foreign policy has not been subject to such wide oscillations as have often been attributed to it. I suggest that the crusading motif has been as much overstated as the isolationist one, that the rhetorical excesses of American bellicosity have matched those of American pacifism, and that the policy actually pursued has been rather consistently set by the pragmatic device of deciding as you go and doing what you seem to have to do.

In the second essay, I analyze the considerations that tend to enter into decisions about reactions to wars in which other states are engaged. For any state, such decisions are crucially important. In the case of such a major power as the United States has become, these decisions have enormous significance for the global system itself. The first clear evidence of America's advancement to the status of a world power was provided by the general acknowledgment that the future of the international system turned upon what the United States decided to do about World War I and, a generation later, about World War II. Americans came to realize the impact of their country upon the world, and the problem of making American foreign policy has never been the same again. Henceforth, policy making is a matter of how to protect and promote the national interest of the United States *and* of how to meet its global responsibilities.

The third essay concentrates on one of the recipes for dealing with wars in the international environment: the doctrine of collective security, which assigns to all states—and especially to great powers—the task of upholding world order against disturbers of the peace. I contend that neither the United States nor any other state has in fact accepted the version of international responsibility described by collective security theory, and discuss some of the reasons for rejection of the formula for policy that lies at the heart of that theory.

In the final analysis, the United States must not choose between, but must learn how to combine, looking after its own interest and serving the general interest of the international system. Somewhere between crusade and withdrawal, between pressing the world to be like us and calling on the world to stop and let us off, between adopting a rigid formula for action in the global arena and insisting on the right to be utterly unpredictable, lies the possibility of a prudent and responsible American approach to world affairs.

PART ONE

Continuity and Change in the American Approach to World Affairs

A familiar theme of the literature about international relations is that the role of the United States in world affairs has undergone frequent and drastic changes in the twentieth century, and that this mutability of policy derives largely from the rather unusual volatility of American public opinion. Stanley Hoffmann, for instance, writes of "the Wilsonian syndrome," characterized by "oscillation from quietism to activism," and making for a "hectic-static approach to international relations."[1] This emphasis upon change occasionally has favorable overtones, as when it is taken to suggest that America's performance is steadily improving as the country "grows up" and its people develop an increasingly mature understanding of international politics. More often, it carries the critical implication that America tends to vacillate to such a degree that it must be regarded as an unpredictable and therefore as an irresponsible and disturbing element in the international system. This proposition is typically tied to the view that the American people have *not* become sophisticated, in the European sense, about foreign affairs; they swing wildly from enthusiastic support for participation in the global system to sullen demands for withdrawal, from pacifism to belligerence, from naive hope to bitter disillusion, thereby making it impossible for their country to function reliably and effectively in that system.

Although this reading of the American record may owe something to the historian's vested interest in discovering, characterizing, and explaining change, it is an entirely plausible interpretation of that record. It is not, however, immune to challenge, for change, like stability, is sometimes more apparent than real. My purpose in this essay is to examine, first, the case for treating the American record in world affairs as a chronicle of fluctuation and, then, the case for regarding it as a relatively steady performance. How variegated has been the American role?

THE THESIS OF AMERICAN VACILLATION

The issue arises only with reference to the twentieth century. It is generally agreed that from the earliest days of independence the United States adopted an isolationist stance, which it then maintained at least through the nineteeth century. Serious students of American foreign policy know that isolationism should not be interpreted literally. The United States was not, and did not purport or attempt to be, entirely cut off from the rest of the world. Its policy was to abstain, so far as possible, from political and military involvement in Europe, the central arena of world politics, avoiding peacetime alliances with European powers so as to escape being exploited and entangled in quarrels not its own. Isolationism represented an effort to capitalize on the advantages of remoteness and moatedness; as Washington explained in his Farewell Address, the policy of isolationism was made possible by the fact of isolation. It was made necessary by the weakness, disunity, and vulnerability that rendered the fledgling state utterly unfit for the strenuous game of power politics. It was made desirable for Americans by their sense of differentiation and moral separation from the European world, their conviction that they had created a fresh and innocent society that could only be sullied by close involvement in European politics.

What is perhaps the standard version of American history has it that this original policy of aloofness, so unchallengeably sensible in the early stages of the country's development, persisted longer than it should have done and that the American people have had difficulty throughout the twentieth century in shaking it off and escaping the nostalgia for the simpler and easier time when it was appropriate. At this point, vacillation begins. The abandonment of the isolationist position in response to the recognition that America is no longer isolated but is inescapably at the center of world affairs, and that it has become a great power whose action or inaction may have decisive impact upon the entire world, has been a process of fits and starts. The conventional view is that the United States has, with popular support, emerged from isolationism to play an active international role as a major power, but has periodically retreated from that new role, under popular pressure for retrenchment. Participation in World War I and sponsorship of the creation of the League of Nations were followed by two decades of isolationism. America resumed the internationalist role in World War II and the period of constructing international organizations and alliances that followed the war, but shifted again toward isolationism in response to the trauma of Vietnam. Thus, a pattern of fluctuation between isolationism and internationalism (or interventionism), between lethargy and hyperactivity, is discerned.

Another interpretation of America's twentieth-century record, which I prefer, differs from the above mainly in that it identifies a third position, between isolationism and internationalism, which I would describe as that of the auxiliary. The player of the auxiliary role is neither determined to remain aloof from international political and military struggles nor committed to become involved, but is intent upon retaining the freedom to choose entry into and withdrawal from those struggles. The role entails sporadic and temporary intrusion into the arena; it is that of the relief pitcher or pinch hitter. As Abraham Flexner put it in 1922: "I can't help thinking that in the long run we shall be able to help most if we keep out [of the League of Nations], throwing our weight into the scale from time to time whenever a specific good can be accomplished thereby."[2]

I think it is fair to argue that the United States did not shift from consistent adherence to isolationism in the nineteenth century to confused alternation between isolationism and internationalism in the twentieth century, but that it first moved from isolationism to the auxiliary position. This shift began by the turn of the century, and it is clear that President Theodore Roosevelt envisaged the United States as a powerful and important auxiliary player in world politics. This country entered World War I as an auxiliary, intent on sending the boys "over there" to determine the outcome of the struggle and then on "bringing the boys back home." Before the war was won, President Wilson had concluded that it was essential for world peace and for America's welfare that this country move from the auxiliary to the internationalist role, that of the firmly committed and reliably permanent leader in world affairs; the League of Nations was intended by Wilson and by his British and French counterparts as the vehicle for such American leadership. Those who defeated this Wilsonian project in the United States were not, in the main, isolationists. Rather, they were proponents of the retention of the auxiliary position; they were committed to uncommittedness, to maintenance of the free hand in foreign policy that would enable America to decide for itself whether, when, and where to throw its weight into the scales of international politics.

A case might be made for the view that the auxiliary role that had been reaffirmed after World War I was briefly abandoned after 1935 when the isolationist "never again" mood prevailed in an America that saw a new European war in the offing. In the early phases of that war, however, the notion of the United States as an "arsenal of democracy," a supplier of equipment and a reserve force that might ultimately be required to prevent an Axis victory, suggested a return to the position of the auxiliary.

Once the United States entered the struggle, there came a revival of the Wilsonian view that only the sustained participation of this country in international politics could save the world from recurrent and disastrous disorder. This time, the effort to induce America to go beyond the role of the auxiliary to that of the dependable leader was successful. The United Nations (UN) and the North Atlantic Treaty Organization (NATO) have generally been regarded as the most important symbols and embodiments of that success. The UN appeared as the new League of Nations, this time not abandoned by its American creators but accepted by them as the essential vehicle for their country's exercise of its heavy responsibility for the ordering of the international system. NATO, billed as America's first peacetime military alliance, would have been less acceptable to Wilson but it dramatized even more clearly than the UN the conversion of the United States to the role of resolute chief of international resistance to disturbers of world peace. The United States had asserted its repudiation of the long-cherished right to be unpredictable and had made an unprecedented commitment to committedness as the means of forestalling international disorder. It had at last accepted the role that Wilson had urged upon it some twenty-five years earlier.

Whether the shift made by the United States in the years immediately after World II is interpreted as the decisive abandonment of isolationism or as the dropping of the auxiliary role, it is almost universally regarded as the great turning point in the history of America's relationship with the rest of the world. The subsequent international performance of the United States is subject to widely differing characterizations. On the one hand, America has been praised for devoted global service and responsible leadership; taking an enlightened view of its national interest, the United States has made itself, according to this view, a bulwark of order, stability, and freedom. On the other hand, the charge of wicked, ruthless imperialism has been raised; seeking global hegemony, the United States has become, in this version, a bulwark of oppressive regimes throughout the world. In either case, good or evil, wise or foolish, the United States has been regarded as a prominent and frequently dominant leader in the international system.

It is clear that the leadership career of the United States was significantly interrupted in the late 1960s and early 1970s, in consequence of what happened in Vietnam and, perhaps more importantly, of what happened in the United States about Vietnam. Whether they developed a mood of repentance for national evildoing or of weariness in national welldoing, Americans emerged from the trauma of Vietnam disillusioned about the role or the plight of the leader in world affairs and intent upon limiting the American commitment to such a role. Some were charged with having reverted to isolationism, and some claimed to have done so. A great deal of speculation has taken place, both in America and in the world outside, as to whether the United States has abdicated or will abdicate or will return to its leading role in international affairs, and as to the degree to which "neo-isolationism" has taken hold. To one who accepts the validity of the concept of the auxiliary, it would appear most accurate to say that the United States has switched from the internationalist to the auxiliary position. Even those who claim the neo-isolationist label would probably reject as impossible and undesirable a return to nineteenth-century-style aloofness from the central arena of the international system. What they really have in mind, I suspect, is a sharp restriction of commitments that would greatly expand the freedom of the United States to examine each case that might seem to call for American involvement and to decide upon its course of action or inaction by reference to clearly perceived and tangible national interests. This is the position of the auxiliary.

Whether one's analysis includes the notion of the auxiliary or is restricted to the categories of isolationism and internationalism, it appears that the United States considered but rejected the role of international leader in the aftermath of World War I, accepted it in response to World War II, and at the very least became thoroughly ambivalent about it in reaction to Vietnam. This suggests that America's perception of its necessary and proper role in the world has changed quite fundamentally at intervals of about twenty-five years: roughly, in 1920, 1945, and 1970. This is the record that inspires the charge of American unsteadiness in foreign policy and incites Americans to chide each other for being immature, impatient, inexperienced in the ways of power politics, too easily disillusioned, and too much inclined to spasms of energy and spells of apathy in world affairs. (Although the American commentator usually ascribes these faults to "us Americans," it is always understood that he, despite his nationality, is not really included in the indictment;

he, whoever he is, is the one American wise enough to understand the foibles of his countrymen!)

THE THESIS OF AMERICAN STEADINESS

The case for the assertion that the American record in world affairs in the twentieth century has been marked by steadiness rather than vacillation requires a reconsideration of the customary view, expressed above, that the United States made major changes in its approach to participation in international relations in 1945 and again in 1970, to use the approximate dates that I have suggested. Was there a genuine revolution in American foreign policy at the end of World War II, marked by the acceptance of the role of a Great Power (or, indeed, that of a Superpower), of peacetime alliances, and of leadership in multilateral institutions? If so, was that revolution reversed in reaction to Vietnam, so that the United States became again an auxiliary in the global arena? Let us examine the thesis that there was less change on both these occasions than met the eye.

First, I will consider the phenomenon of which NATO has served as the supreme symbol: the formation of a network of peacetime alliances. During the first decade after the end of hostilities in World War II, the United States busied itself in all parts of the world with the establishment of bilateral and multilateral arrangements that, whatever they were called, were intended to function as alliances. Thus, it appeared that, contrary to all American precedent and to the "pinch-hitter" characteristic of the auxiliary role, the United States had on this occasion resolved—and formally announced its intention—to stay in rather than to pull out of the global political arena in the postwar period. The apparent revolution lay in the *postwar engagement* of the United States.

The challenge to the revolutionary thesis begins with the reopening of the question: *Were* NATO, the Rio Pact, CENTO, SEATO, ANZUS, and the cluster of bilateral treaties *peacetime*, that is to say, *postwar*, alliances? The rejection of that thesis entails a negative answer to the question. While the hostilities of World War II had been both formally and actually ended in 1945, the lack of the customary peace conference meant that the legal state of war was not terminated in the usual fashion. But that technicality is of negligible importance; what counts is the fact that, for Americans and not for them alone, the Cold War was a new phase of World War II. Psychologically and politically, if not legally and militarily, it was a continuation of the struggle that had begun with Hitler's invasion of Poland. As the British scholar, Martin Wight, put it, World War II was a conflict of democracies, Fascists, and Communists,

> with each party sometimes drawing nearer one of its rivals than the other. And when a temporary coalition of democracies and Communists had eliminated the Fascists in war, the conflict was simplified into a direct antagonism of the democracies and the Communists, each of them believing the other to be closer to the defeated Fascists than to itself.[3]

The case for this heretical view is clouded by the precipitant demobilization of American forces that followed the defeat of Germany and Japan; that certainly suggested a popular conviction that the war was over and the time had come for return to "normalcy." Throughout the war, however, there had been a not-altogether-dormant conviction in the United States that the Soviet Union was, in the final analysis, not an ally but an enemy. After all, was this not a struggle of the democracies against the totalitarians, and had the Soviet Union not entered the war as an ally of Hitler? This point of view was generally kept beneath the surface of public opinion so long as the fighting continued, because it was considered improper to say anything that might damage military collaboration among the allies, and perhaps because of reluctance to confirm what was a favorite theme of Nazi propaganda: that the Soviet Union was the *real* enemy against which the West ought to be fighting. With the end of the military struggle against the Axis, war weariness prevented any of the victorious peoples from waxing enthusiastic about engaging in a new conflict, and the testing of the possibilities of working out an harmonious relationship with the USSR for the future was a politically necessary undertaking. But the fear that the USSR would turn out to be an enemy not unlike the members of the Axis coalition survived the war and lost little time in emerging after the Japanese surrender. America had hoped for a postwar period. What followed the events of 1945, with hardly a decent interval, was a Cold War that might certainly be construed as the ultimate phase of World War II. From this point of view, World War II was not followed by Cold War, but changed into Cold War.

The implication of this thesis is that NATO and all the other alliances that the United States promoted were not new-fangled peacetime but old-fashioned wartime alliances. The United States had not engaged in an unprecedented postwar retention of its involvement in world affairs, but had simply developed the necessary alliance ties for the continuation of the war in its new, essentially non-military, phase. The Cold War demanded and produced innovative behavior, but it was behavior associated with a wartime, not a postwar, mentality. Hence, the claim that the late 1940s brought a drastic change in America's postwar habits of foreign policy is invalid.

If 1945 did not mark the end of World War II in the political psychology of Americans, when *did* the postwar period begin for them? It is not easy to establish a definite date; perhaps that great struggle petered out in the psychological sense just as it did in the legal sense. One might argue that the war ended when anti-anticommunism set in—when anticommunism lost its moral legitimacy for liberals—and American society began to feel that Communism was a force in the world to be tolerated and lived with more than guarded against and resisted. *Detente*, in short, may be translated as Cold War armistice.

This would suggest that the sense of the war's being finished was emerging from the middle 1960s onward, and 1970 might serve as the rough approximation of the start of the postwar era. This is, of course, the period of the development of the domestic opposition to America's involvement in Vietnam. Seen in this light, that opposition was not a call for the abandonment of an American commitment to peacetime leadership in international politics. Rather, it was simply an expression of the withdrawal syndrome that normally accompanies the ending of an American war. In the American political psyche, World War II, including its Cold War extension, had finally come to a conclusion; now it was time for America to do what it always does at the end of a war—"Bring the boys back home!" It is worth noting the similarity between that traditional slogan and the theme of George McGovern's presidential campaign in 1972: "Come home, America." Because the war was over, it was wrong for the United States to be still fighting in Vietnam. Indeed, in this version, Vietnam became a kind of latter-day Battle of New Orleans, a battle mistakenly fought after the war had been finished, because somebody had failed to get the word. The American people no longer believed that it was necessary or proper to be engaged in a war to block Communist expansionism; they had lost their stomach for it and their commitment to it, and they declared the beginning of a postwar period.

If this analysis is valid, the United States did not first undertake, and then abandon, a commitment to international military and political leadership in peacetime. Instead, Americans treated World War II and the Cold War as a single protracted war and when they concluded—not in 1945, but at about the beginning of the 1970s—that the war was over, they exhibited the usual urge to withdraw from the international arena.

Setting aside the question of when Americans switched from the wartime to the postwar mood, let us return to 1945, when military action against the Axis powers ended and the United States appeared to accept for the indefinite future the role of a major participant in international politics, bearing a heavy responsibility for using its power in support of world order. I refer particularly to the part that this country played in the creation of the United Nations and to the fact that the United States promptly and with apparent enthusiasm joined the new organization. It has been customary to assert that Wilson won in 1945 the battle that he had lost after World War I, his effort to persuade Americans to give up the auxiliary role for the position of leadership in an organized system for safeguarding the order of the world and the security of its constituent states. As I wrote in 1971, the League of Nations had become "the symbol of the folly and irresponsibility of the United States, of America's relinquishment of the task that only it could have performed," and "the United Nations became the symbol of America's repentance, its enlightenment as to what was required for maintaining world order, and its determination to undertake the responsibility that it had previously spurned!"[4]

The formation of the network of alliances that the United States undertook within a few years after joining the United Nations was in at least a theoretical sense inconsistent with the commitment to a collective security scheme of the Wilsonian sort, but it nevertheless tended to reinforce the notion that the United States had firmly resolved to remain permanently at the center of the international political stage; whether as the chief actor in the new world organization or as the main defender of its partners in alliance, America was committed to vigilance and decisive action when required to uphold world order against aggression.

This interpretation of America's approach to world affairs in the aftermath of World War II leads to the contention that the United States reverted to its earlier form in the aftermath of Vietnam. In this view, the trauma of that involvement incited Americans to insist upon the reduction of commitments and the curtailment of the role that their country had played for some twenty-five years. Henceforth, the United States would choose its engagements with care; its previous open-ended commitment to police the world now seemed not responsible but reckless. In future, the role of the United States would be improvised, not institutionalized. It would, in short, again be that of the auxiliary. Thus, in one brief generation, the radical transformation of America's international performance had been radically reversed.

Let us consider a reading of the postwar record of the United States that challenges this entire line of thought. Did Americans change their collective mind in 1945, and change it back in 1970—or did they never change it at all? Did the United States decide, in reaction to Vietnam, that its commitment to the role of a great power in presiding over world order had been a mistake—or did it discover that that commitment had been an illusion?

The issue turns in large part on the meaning to be attached to American acceptance of membership in the United Nations. Did that act really mean that the United States had accepted, for the indefinite future, the responsibility to uphold world order? This should not be too readily assumed, given the American tradition of regarding international organizations as *substitutes*, rather than as vehicles, for national action in support of world order. For instance, the legalistic approach to world peace that dominated American thought before World War I emphasized the order-keeping responsibility of some sort of world court; the task was not to be assumed by the United States and other states, but was to be assigned to a panel of judges. After World War II, the considerable attractiveness of the idea of world federalism to Americans may well have derived from its promise to invent a globe-dominating Superpower that would take over the management of world affairs, relieving states of that onerous responsibility; the United States, along with other countries, could let that Colossal George do it! The United States, perhaps no more but certainly no less than other states, has been inclined to long for a *deus ex machina* rather than to concentrate on the question: how should we states organize ourselves to do what we have to do for the stability of our system?

The theory of collective security does focus on that question, rejecting as illusion the notion that order can be provided *for* states; it insists, uncompromisingly, that order will be produced by states, or not at all. This does not increase its political appeal, and the Achilles heel of a collective security system is, indeed, the fact that it must rely upon states to enforce order. But the great strength of collective security theory lies in the fact that it recognizes this necessity. It does not pretend, or nourish the illusion, that there is an alternative.

The issue is whether the United States, in planning its future after World War II, genuinely resolved to carry the burden of responsibility for world order that collective security theory assigns to such a powerful state as America had become. It appeared to have done so. Not that the United Nations Charter was the blueprint for a thoroughgoing system of collective security; for one thing, the veto in the Security Council meant that the United States could not be pressed to act in support of world order unless it chose to do so. Moreover, American alliance treaties were equipped with escape clauses that preserved national freedom to decide how to react to challenges. But the issue is not whether the United States came to be legally obligated to act in defense of world order, or of the security of its allies. It is, rather, whether the United States had developed the political determination to do so, whether it had become committed, to *itself*, to play the role implied by its position in the UN and in its system of alliances. Had the American approach to world affairs really been transformed as it appeared to have been?

Skepticism about that transformation ought perhaps to be stimulated by acknowledgment of the tendency of states, including the United States, to make commitments without having considered the possible costs of fulfilling them and having clearly resolved to pay those costs if the occasion should arise. As I have argued elsewhere,[5] Wilson's enthusiasm for having the United States promise to take the lead in the enforcement of the no-aggression rule that is central to collective security theory did not seem to be matched by seriousness about doing what the promise required, and there is legitimate uncertainty about whether the United States, in joining the UN, was making a carefully calculated and seriously accepted commitment or a casual one. It is clear that the United States changed after World War II in at least one sense: it accepted the view that *committedness* has value, that being thought to be committed is useful for deterrence. But had Americans really become committed to commitment, or only to its appearance? Had they accepted the costs that go with the benefits of commitment?

The answer turns in some measure on the degree of confidence that deterrence theory inspired in Americans. Deterrence must not be founded upon a bluff—but, if it succeeds, one's bluff is never called. Wilson did not overcome American opposition to membership in the League by his argument that the best way to avoid involvement in war was to promise that we would go to war whenever aggression occurred, but it is quite possible that Americans were more impressed after World War II by the utility of the deterrent threat than by the necessity of doing what had been threatened, if the threat should fail to deter. The more confidence one has in the effectiveness of the promise, the less one needs to worry about the costs that will be incurred if the promise should prove ineffective.

One is reminded of the admission made in 1966 by Senator J. William Fulbright that when he had supported the ratification of the Southeast Asia Treaty and the protocol extending its protection to South Vietnam, "I did not anticipate . . . that this was a serious matter, I mean anything like it is. I thought it was just one other country among many to whom we were giving aid, and I really never became concerned about this matter until about the time of the Bay of Tonkin, and I paid no particular attention to it. . . ."[6] I strongly suspect that many Americans, ranging from private citizens to high officials of government, have endorsed solemn commitments in such a light-hearted mood as Fulbright described.

Vietnam provided a painful reminder that to be committed is to incur the cost as well as to acquire the advantage of commitment. America could seem to be firmly committed, so long as it did not have to pay the bills for commitment; when the bills started coming in, America found that it had not really accepted the responsibility for action that it had affirmed so blithely. In this situation, the idea of the UN as a vehicle for American leadership gave way to the notion that the organization might act instead of the United States. Hubert Humphrey, Democratic candidate for president, asserted during the 1968 campaign that "The United States cannot play the role of global gendarme. The American people don't want it, and the rest of the world won't accept it. . . . But the alternative to American peacekeeping . . . must be peacekeeping by the United Nations or by regional agencies."[7] His victorious opponent, Richard Nixon, was reported soon after his inauguration as being disposed "to shy from unilateral entanglements and rely more on international organizations to police the peace and good order of the world."[8]

Did America retreat from a commitment or discover that it had really never made one? The answer depends upon whether one defines commitment as external obligation or as internal resolution. The United States, I would argue, had affirmed certain obligations without developing the resolution to back them up. It had not always meant what it had said; it had believed that it was willing to play a role that, in the moment of truth, it would find it had never seriously contemplated—because, Fulbright-like, it had "paid no particular attention to it." Vietnam, I believe, did not so much induce America to change its mind as force it to come to know its own mind. Commitment, construed as dedication to a line of behavior, had not been there.

What America discovered about itself during the turmoil of the intervention in Vietnam it might well have learned much earlier. The United States has an habitual tendency to assume a posture without taking up a position, to state an intention without forming a resolution. We might trace this tendency as far back as the Monroe Doctrine; it certainly appeared a century later in the Kellogg-Briand Pact, which enabled this country to speak out against aggressive war without resolving to do anything about it. More to the point, the leadership career of the United States after World War II has included such episodes as the backing away from the 1947 UN plan for partition of Palestine as soon as it became evident that the plan would encounter armed resistance from the Arab world, the denial in advance of the intention to respond militarily to such a crisis as occurred in Korea in 1950, the confusing of Britain and France as to American willingness to support a military response to the Suez crisis of 1956, and the ambivalent behavior of this country in the Bay of Pigs and Iranian hostage cases. One might note also that George Kennan wrote vigorously about containment but shied away from any implication of military means for achieving that objective, and that John Foster Dulles talked bravely about liberation and rollback but was ready with assurances that he did not have in mind the use of force! This record suggests that from the very beginning of the postwar period—that is, well before the Vietnamese engagement became troublesome—the United States had grave misgivings about military involvements and was extremely reluctant to take action in real-life situations, as distinguished from threatening or promising action in hypothetical situations. Quasi-pacifism has been persistently in competition with firmness and vigilance, and insistence upon freedom to tailor policy to circumstances has contended with commitment to predictable reaction to disturbances of world order.

Such caution, uncertainty, and hesitation are not peculiarly American traits. Indeed, this is the story of the collective security project everywhere in the twentieth century. People who think and say that they support collective security and accept its obligations turn out, in the crunch, to be either quasi-pacifists, opposed to fighting for high-minded, idealistic reasons, or nationalists, lacking a sense of global responsibility and insistent upon retaining national discretion to react to disorders as circumstances may seem to warrant. Commitment to collective security seems always to be a matter of hoping for its benefits without genuinely accepting its costs. The whole world, not just the United States, faces the paradox that the danger to survival posed by modern war inspires the recognition both of the need to be reliably willing and able to fight against disturbers of the peace and of the need to avoid becoming involved in fighting if at all possible.

That sort of ambivalence seems to me to have characterized the mood of the United States throughout the postwar period; Vietnam intensified but did not introduce it. It is the mood of the auxiliary, feeling free to make choices, and obliged to make carefully calculated ones, about intervention in international conflicts. The conclusion is therefore emerging that the United States did not change its conception of its international role in 1945 and change back to its earlier view in 1970 or thereabouts; it only thought that it had changed after World War II. In reality, America has remained, throughout the twentieth century, in the role of auxiliary—acting in world affairs when and as it thinks necessary to uphold interests and values that concern it, acknowledging no obligation to be systematic about this but treasuring the right to be unpredictable even when it hopes that its deterrent threats and reassuring guarantees will seem credible.

This conclusion does not support the proposition that America's twentieth-century record in world affairs has been one of vacillation, except in the sense that the auxiliary role entails episodic involvement in events. It says that America has steadily adhered to the position that it will act pragmatically, and therefore variably, in the global arena— even when it has purported to accept, and has believed that it has accepted, commitments that bind it to act otherwise. Indeed, one might argue that this has *always* been the position of the United States. Isolationism was always more doctrine than practice, and even the doctrine was more heavily qualified than its absolutist-sounding label intimated. Doctrines both of aloofness and of commitment to involvement have served to mislead, to mask the actual pragmatism of American foreign policy; the United States has talked "Never" and "Always," but has practiced "Sometimes."

The ultimate implication of this analysis is that, throughout its history as an independent state, the United States has functioned as an auxiliary player in the international system. Before World War I, it was a relatively unimportant auxiliary, and Americans found few occasions when they thought they could or should act in international relations. The rarely active auxiliary could be called, with some justification, an isolationist. Its intrusions into both the world wars of this century established the new stature of this country, and since World War II the United States has been a highly important auxiliary, frequently but not invariably finding it possible and desirable to throw its weight into the management of international affairs. This is to say that America has become a far more active participant in international affairs—indeed, a leader—but it is nonetheless an auxiliary: a participant committed above all to retaining its freedom to decide on action or inaction, in accordance with its own judgment of circumstances and of the interests and values at stake in the events that claim its attention.

NOTES

[1]*Gulliver's Troubles, Or the Setting of American Foreign Policy* (New York: McGraw-Hill, 1968), pp. 191, 380.
[2]Quoted in Raymond B. Fosdick, *Letters on the League of Nations* (Princeton: Princeton University Press, 1966), p. 136.
[3]*Power Politics*, edited by Hedley Bull and Carstan Holbraad (Harmondsworth, Middlesex: Penguin Books, 1979), p. 86.
[4]Inis L. Claude, Jr., "The Symbolic Significance of the United Nations," *The Virginia Quarterly Review*, Autumn 1971, pp. 490–491.
[5]Inis L. Claude, Jr., "Casual Commitment in International Relations," *Political Science Quarterly,* Fall 1981, pp. 367–379.
[6]J. William Fulbright, *The Vietnam Hearings* (New York: Random House, Vintage Books Edition, 1966), p. 42.
[7]From a speech delivered in San Francisco on September 26, 1968. Text in *The Washington Post*, September 27, 1968, p. A6.
[8]"Let Us . . . Go Forward Together," *Newsweek*, January 27, 1969, p. 19.

PART TWO

What to Do About Other People's Wars

War is a persistent feature of the international system. At any given time it is likely that at least one armed conflict is going on. Most of these directly involve a limited number of states, which is to say that "other people's wars" are much more common than "our wars." Every state is regularly—almost constantly—confronted with the fact that wars not immediately involving itself are being waged, and with the necessity of deciding what, if anything, it should do about them.

This essay is devoted to an examination of this problem of foreign policy. I shall be concerned mainly with decisions about how to react to international wars, although civil wars will be considered when intervention has appeared to transform them into conflicts between the state in difficulty and another intent upon exacerbating and exploiting that state's internal problems. I shall exclude consideration of decisions either to initiate a war or to respond to direct attack; in short, this study concerns the role of *third* parties, not that of the first or the second party, in armed conflicts. I shall give special although not exclusive attention to the reactions of the United States to other people's wars.

This problem of policy is typically a difficult one, fraught with controversy over its moral, legal, and political aspects. What a state should do, what it can do, what it can afford to do, what it can afford not to do—all such questions about response to wars between other states are troublesome for the statesman, both in the sense that he may have difficulty in forming a wise decision and in the sense that whatever decision he makes is likely to arouse sharp disagreement and passionate argument within the state. The hottest foreign policy issue confronted by President Washington concerned the appropriate American response to war between France and Britain; the question that President Reagan most carefully evaded in his televised debate about foreign policy with

Walter Mondale during the 1984 presidential campaign had to do with the identification of states in whose defense the United States would resort to military action. We might recall that Presidents Wilson and Franklin Roosevelt ran for reelection in 1916 and 1940 boasting of having kept this country out of the current European war and offering the hope, if not the promise, of continuing that policy—and that, in both cases, they subsequently took the United States into war. For today's generation, the traumas of Korea and Vietnam provide a guarantee that consideration of reaction to other people's wars by the United States will be a matter of the greatest political sensitivity.

The difficulty of these decisions is in large part a reflection of their importance to the state that makes them; its security, even its survival, may depend upon the wisdom of its reactions to wars. Moreover, the entire international system may be fundamentally affected by what states do or fail to do about wars not immediately involving themselves. Obviously, the reactions of major states such as the United States or the USSR have the greatest impact upon the global system. Let us look at the choices that are available, and at the factors that may enter into the decisions of states.

THE RANGE OF CHOICE

(1) Keeping One's Distance

The first option is to stay out of, to stand aside from, a war in which two or more other states are engaged. The objective of this policy is not so much to affect the war (except in the sense that not joining in the struggle contributes to the limitation of its scope) as to avoid being affected by it. One sees the conflict, quite literally, as *other people's* war—not our business. Non-involvement is, of course, a matter of degree. At its extreme, this policy entails simply ignoring the war, paying little or no attention to it. This may be thought difficult in the age of global communications, but the media are notoriously selective; a war that is not, for whatever reason, seriously reported by television and the press makes a noise comparable to that of the legendary tree that falls in an uninhabited forest. Moreover, most of the people of most states have quite limited curiosity about what is going on in the farthest reaches of the planet. Whenever a scholar or journalist displays a list of "wars now in progress," even well-informed people are likely to discover some items of which they have been unaware.

The possibility of ignoring a war depends on such factors as its location, its size, and the identity of the belligerent states. That possibility varies, too, with the identity of the third party in question. A great power, almost by definition, considers itself to have—and is considered by other states to have—interests and responsibilities throughout the world, and is therefore unlikely to display the inattentiveness to any war that one might expect from, say, Costa Rica with respect to a war between Burundi and Botswana. Membership in the United Nations tends to make pseudo-great powers of even the smallest states, in the sense that it encourages and enables them to pose as having policies relating to virtually all international events and issues, but in truth many of the world's states have little occasion to pay serious attention to most wars outside their own neighborhoods. Not every war attracts the notice even of such globally active states as the United States and the Soviet Union.

America's traditional policy of isolationism with respect to European politics reflected the urge to take advantage of the fact that the Atlantic separated the New World from the Old. Being isolated from the main arena of international politics, the United States might succeed in maintaining a policy of aloofness from the conflicts endemic to that arena. Isolationism was not a matter of ignoring European wars, but of deliberately and warily keeping one's distance.

The least stringent of the policies of aloofness is that of neutrality, which entails the effort by a third party to maintain a special relationship with both sides engaged in a war, a relationship defined by rather elaborate rules. While observance of the duties of neutrality tends to keep the neutral state at a distance from the conflict, insistence upon the rights accompanying that status may pull the neutral into the maelstrom. Those Americans who were most adamantly resolved to keep the United States out of the European war that was first threatening and then occurring in the late 1930s came to recognize that the exercise of neutral rights endangered their goal, and therefore urged a return to the unyielding aloofness of isolationism. In the end, of course, those who favored the renunciation of neutral duties by the United States triumphed over those who called for the abandonment of neutral rights.

As we shall see, powerful arguments are raised in today's circumstances to the effect that states neither can nor should stand aside from military conflicts. Realistically, it is contended, states cannot expect to withstand the centripetal force of such disturbances; moreover, the argument runs, their own interest in national security and world order dictates active concern rather than passive observation when violence erupts in the world. Although these contentions purport to refer to states-in-general, it is evident that they are addressed primarily to the more powerful members of the multistate system. Countering these arguments is the nearly universal dread of war, the sense that military engagement has become intolerably dangerous, a sentiment that often inspires the insistence that one's state should have as little as possible to do with other people's wars. Avoidance of war is also sometimes linked—or confused—with prevention; staying out of a conflict may be represented as casting a vote against war, and therefore as supremely responsible behavior.

A number of factors make the policy of aloofness especially attractive to the United States. Although the shrinkage of distance in the twentieth century has diminished the American sense of remoteness, the remnant of that sense combines with the fact that international war has not yet been fought on the American mainland to keep alive the notion that the United States has a genuine choice about involvement in wars. Knowledge that war can, in principle, be brought home to Americans is at least partially offset by the paucity of such experience, and by the implausibility of the idea that most wars, regardless of where they occur, pose a significant threat to the security of the United States. Unlike Europeans, who are accustomed to being overrun by war, Americans *go* to war; they see war as something that happens "over there"—and that their country can choose to enter or to avoid. Remember the only half facetious slogan that had currency among critics of American involvement in Vietnam: "What if they gave a war and nobody came?"

The American urge to choose abstention has the advantage of legitimacy derived from tradition established by the Founding Fathers. Isolationism fell into disrepute during World War II, but disillusion with the results of American activity on the international scene appears to have restored some of the appeal of that doctrine. Aloofness from other people's wars has a claim to intellectual respectability in the United States that it lacks in other major powers.

This tendency to stand aside is reinforced by American exceptionalism, which stresses the moral rather than the geographical distance between the New World and the Old. The virtue of the American system is contrasted with the depravity of the rest of the world, and avoidance of unnecessary entanglement in the corrupt affairs of the Bad Old System is the recipe for preservation of innocence. President Wilson's failure to entice the United States into the League of Nations may be interpreted as his failure to convince the country that the League really was, as he insisted, a new and morally superior international system, worthy of American participation. The exceptionalist is inclined to view the world out there as engaged in a nefarious and dangerous game that America ought to avoid.

Strangely enough, the recent revival of the disposition of Americans toward isolationism appears to have been fueled at least as much by cynicism about their own society as by cynicism about the outside world. Vietnam and Watergate are no doubt major contributors to a mood of pessimism that encourages the expectation that the United States can do no right: it is invincibly inclined to support unworthy causes, so that only inaction will save it from improper action, and it is incorrigibly inclined to botch whatever it attempts in international affairs, so that only inaction will save it from debacle. This decline in self-confidence about both the morality and the effectiveness of the United States as a leader in the world may well be temporary, but it increases the appeal of the "let's stay at home and mind our own business" motif at least for the moment.

Finally, the avoidance of involvement in other people's wars is made attractive by the strong probability of serious political divisions among Americans about the nature and direction of their country's involvement. From George Washington's day to Ronald Reagan's, controversy has raged as to which party at war should have American support, or whether either should have it. Such disagreement lies at the root of the pessimistic mood that I described above; the conviction that the United States will always support the Bad Guys is the refuge of those who have lost a political battle, those who disagree with the direction of policy that has been adopted. Ethnic cleavages in the American population have sometimes been considered responsible for divisions about policy towards wars, as have partisan and ideological differences. The United States is probably not, however, abnormally deficient in national solidarity on matters of foreign policy; what is unusual is the openness of the American political system, its provision of opportunities for belligerent governments to intrude into the process by which public and governmental opinion is formed and the direction of foreign policy is determined. Deciding what to do about other people's wars is the occasion for political struggle in the United States. President Washington concluded that the best way to avoid inflaming factionalism was to decide that neither party to a war should enjoy American support. That advice still holds; the quagmire to be dreaded may lie not in Vietnam, or in El Salvador, but in Washington. Standing aside from a war tends to appear to the United States as a way of avoiding sin, danger, loss, embarrassment, and—not least—internal discord.

(2) Stopping the War

The second possible objective of the bystanding state is that of contributing to the interruption of a war that has begun between other states. Again, the third party is intent upon staying out of the war, but its policy of abstention is, in this case, active rather than passive; retaining the goal of being as little affected by the war as possible, it tries to act upon the war—to limit, contain, and shorten it, to induce the parties to call it off.

The pursuit of this objective may entail either or both of two distinguishable but related types of activity. The first is that of bringing persuasion and pressure to bear upon one or both of the belligerent parties. Third states may act unilaterally or multilaterally, in improvised groups or through established organizations, to impress upon the warring states their concern about the danger posed by the outbreak of violence and their demand that efforts at negotiating a peaceful settlement be made. Pressure may be exerted by resolutions deploring resort to hostilities, by diplomatic representations behind the scenes, and even by the manipulation of threats and promises concerning various forms of aid to the states involved. In this kind of activity, major powers obviously have greater weight than minor ones; American pressure to stop fighting is likely to be more effective than, say, Burmese pressure. Moreover, a great power's involvement in an alliance with one or both sides may be an advantage. The role of the United States in restraining military action by Israél has been so prominent for a generation that Israeli leaders consider it necessary to achieve whatever objective they may seek very quickly, in anticipation of America's blowing the whistle, and the Arab world has developed mixed feelings about the American alliance with Israel, weighing the ally's restraint of Israel against its support of that state. It is easy to exaggerate the capacity of a powerful ally to control the belligerent tendencies of client states, or the capacity of the organized international system to induce states to refrain from violence, but pressures from other states to cease fire and seek nonmilitary solutions to their quarrels may substantially reduce the incidence of international violence.

The second form of war-stopping activity is the provision of assistance to the parties in reaching agreement on a peaceful settlement or at least the cessation of fighting. The notions that third parties are entitled to offer their services to quarreling states and that they may be able to play an indispensable role in facilitating agreement are staples of twentieth-century doctrine. Services such as mediation, conciliation, arbitration, impartial fact-finding, observation of cease-fire lines, and provision of peacekeeping military personnel may enable hostile states to come to terms. Acting either within or outside the framework of international organizations, states frequently undertake by such means to promote the termination of wars. The third-party role is usually conceived as preeminently that of the relatively weak state whose neutrality in matters of power politics is clearly established, and states in that category sometimes make outstanding contributions to the patching up of the international peace. In some instances, however, states that are among the most powerful and the most prominently engaged participants in international political struggles devote themselves to giving pacific-settlement assistance; one thinks, for instance, of the Soviet role in mediating between India and Pakistan in 1965, and of American involvement in recurrent negotiations for solution or management of Arab-Israeli conflicts and for settlement of the Namibian question. Every state, from the greatest to the smallest, may find on some occasion that it is in a good position to help two or more other states back away from military conflict.

We must view with caution, however, the assumption that all states are unequivocally committed to the ideal of minimizing armed conflict among other states. It is true that the formal rhetoric of statesmen decries war as an unmitigated evil and urges all states to live in peace, and most political leaders probably do regard war, in the abstract, as a disturbance of international stability that adversely affects the interests of their own states. But war consists of *wars*, and statesmen are much more discriminating in their appraisal of and reaction to wars than their blanket deploring of war would suggest. They know, for instance, that wars are not equally dangerous to the global system or equally likely to ignite a general conflagration. Statesmen throughout the world would be greatly alarmed by the outbreak of hostilities between the Soviet

Union and Poland, but would be less disturbed by a clash between Burundi and Rwanda. Indeed, a state may regard a particular war as favorable to its own interests, welcoming the preoccupation of the belligerents with their struggle and the possible weakening of one or both sides, or looking forward to the possible effects of the victory of one and the defeat of the other. It is not clear, for example, that the Soviet Union was distressed by the long and costly entanglement of the United States in the Vietnam War, or that conflicts among Arab states are disadvantageous to Israel. The hope of states that they may profit from, or be able to take advantage of, the wars of other states is not uniformly overshadowed by their fear of catastrophe triggered by such wars.

The incentive of third parties to bring about the cessation of a particular war depends heavily upon their attitude toward the status quo that the war promises or threatens to alter. Depending upon the timing of such a move, an effort to bring about peace may have the effect either of supporting or of opposing change. It may be, in short, tantamount to taking sides. In the case of a war of aggression, which may be defined as one launched to force acceptance of a change desired by one side and opposed by the other, to demand peace before the aggressor has gained the upper hand is in fact to call for the victory of the defender. In such a case, the aggressor may be identified as the party who loses, who fails to achieve his objective, if the war is interrupted. Thus, from the Arab point of view, calling off the generation-long struggle in the Middle East amounts to declaring Israel the winner; Sadat seemed a traitor to the Arab cause because he deserted the collective effort to deny Israel's claim to statehood in the Middle East. In other instances, the demand for peace may be a call for cessation of resistance, for acquiescence in the triumph of a party that has resorted to coercive measures to effect change. Those who urged American withdrawal from the hostilities in Vietnam demanded, in effect if not always in intent, that Hanoi be permitted to conquer and absorb South Vietnam. Critics of Britain's delayed riposte to Argentina's military entry into the Falkland Islands in 1982 advocated, consciously or not, victory for Argentina. To put it bluntly, peace is sometimes less a noble ideal than a political stratagem. To seek a ceasefire may be not to advocate a neutral and mutually advantageous solution to the underlying conflict but to promote the fulfillment of the aims of one party and the frustration of those of its opponent. How eager a state is to stop a war between others may depend upon the answer to the question: who wins if the war is not fought to a finish?

(3) Playing Favorites

The third choice open to states is to take sides. As I have noted, promoting the premature ending of a war may have, and may be intended to have, unneutral consequences. For that matter, the same is true of standing aloof; non-participation, especially on the part of major powers, affects the outcome of wars. But I refer here to the policy of joining, in some way and to some degree, in more or less open support of one side or the other: converting *their* war into *our* war. Involvement may be confined to verbal endorsement of one cause and condemnation of the other, perhaps accompanied by appropriate voting in international organizations. It may include economic assistance and the provision of military equipment and advice. It may even extend to active military participation. A variety of means is available to states, and especially to such giants as the United States and the Soviet Union, that wish to contribute to the victory of their favorites. The freedom of states to decide about whether, when, and how to become directly involved in conflicts that began as other people's wars is frequently far less than perfect and may on occasion be illusory; engagement in armed struggle is sometimes attributable less to a state's policy than to its predicament. Nevertheless, the question of taking sides is a source of recurrent difficulty for states. Governments and peoples do have important decisions to make on this matter.

Human beings, from ordinary citizens to strategic planners and senior statesmen, are subject to a powerful inclination to favor one side or the other in most wars. War is, among other things, a spectator sport; just as it is difficult to watch a football game without becoming in some measure a fan of one of the teams, so it is hard to remain an utterly dispassionate observer of two sides at war. The urge to "tilt," if not to jump into the fray, is strengthened by the growing sense of interdependence, which suggests that "other people's war" is a misnomer, that any war is everybody's war because every state has a stake in the outcome. It is reinforced as well by the almost universal conviction that the momentous consequences of modern war invest it with enormous moral significance. Taking war as a fit object of moral judgment, one finds it almost impossible to refrain from comparing the positions of the belligerents and opting to express, in some fashion, preference for one or the other. Remaining neutral in thought and spirit as well as in formal status has become no easier since President Wilson proposed it to Americans during the early stages of World War I.

On the other hand, states have strong incentives to avoid involvement of any kind that might lead to their engagement in hostilities. Most states most of the time do not conform to the Hobbesian image; they are not military machines, straining for action, itching for a fight, and dedicated to the conduct of the war of all against all. Their inclination to fight is variable, sporadic, and uncertain. Generally, while states may not object to others' fighting, they are deeply reluctant to fight; the belligerence of the modern national society is more likely to require stimulation than sedation.

Quasi-pacifism, the deep-seated conviction that war must be avoided unless involvement becomes absolutely necessary, is not uniformly spread throughout the world, but it is a powerful force in many areas, certainly including the United States. It is reflected in the "too little—too late" syndrome, and in the recurrent phenomenon of appeasement. Neville Chamberlain's performance at Munich has been subjected to much retrospective criticism, but he acted, however unwisely, for a country that was desperately anxious to avoid war. A statesman who emulated Chamberlain today in the United States would be widely acclaimed as a sensible guardian of the peace, and one who acted as Chamberlain should have done, according to his critics, would seem a reckless courter of disaster.

The passion for avoiding armed conflict lies at the root of the difficulty of inducing states, singly or collectively, to impose any but the most perfunctory sanctions, even when they convict other states of aggression or other misbehavior. This is an era of formal condemnation, hand-wringing, and wrist-slapping, not of concerted military action to ensure the frustration of a state that is regarded as having improperly attacked its neighbor. A shrewd aggressor will cloak his aggression in ambiguity, not to avoid giving eager sanctioners a clear occasion for acting but to help reluctant sanctioners find an excuse for refraining from action. While there is enough bellicosity scattered among the states to produce an abundance of wars of aggression, there is not enough of it concentrated in the global system to fuel the operation of a reliable aggression-control scheme. When it comes to maintaining global order by fighting to defend other states, the members of the international system are more likely to exhibit the Kitty Genovese syndrome, which derives its name from an episode in 1964 in which a number of people stood by passively while a woman was murdered, than to behave as Good Samaritans. The ostensibly prudent urge not to get involved is as powerful a motive in modern international life as in modern urban life.

The appeal of quasi-pacifism is indicated by the degree to which virtuous international behavior is defined negatively rather than positively. We emphasize the propriety of restraint, the avoidance of unwarranted action, rather than that of responsibility, the performance of required action. When has one heard international law invoked to condemn the failure of a state to do its duty? What state was chastized in the court of world opinion for failing to help South Vietnam resist conquest? Does the legal obligation of the United States to defend El Salvador receive as much attention as its legal obligation to refrain from improper action against Nicaragua? The normative bias of current thinking about international affairs tends to support the prudential urge to refrain from direct involvement in other people's wars. The clash between the inclination to take sides and the incentives to stand aside lies at the heart of some of the most difficult decisions that statesmen have to make.

(4) Betting on the Winner

The final possibility to be considered is that states not involved in a war will try not so much to influence as to anticipate its outcome. Remaining outside the conflict, they may pick the probable winner and take special precautions to remain on good terms with that party. In that case, calculations focus not on who *should* win, and should therefore be helped, but on who *will* win, and should therefore be courted. Small states are particularly likely to exhibit this version of the "getting on the bandwagon" syndrome, but even major powers may be affected by it. For instance, domestic critics of the American "tilt" toward Pakistan in that state's conflict with India in 1971 relied in part upon the argument that it was indiscreet to be associated with the party that was clearly destined to be the loser.

It is interesting to note that the tendency of states to bet on the winner conflicts with the expectation of balance of power theorists that states will incline (and their advice that states should incline) to the weaker side in an international conflict, recognizing the aggrandizement of the more powerful as a threat to their security. Note that American political leaders have often expressed the fear that conspicuous Soviet triumphs might induce many other states to join the Soviet camp—not, obviously, to remedy its weakness but to defer to its strength. Rats are not attracted to sinking ships.

The crucial consideration for a state is the degree to which it is able and willing to affect the outcome of a war. If it is willing to enter the struggle, and believes itself capable of having a significant effect upon the outcome, it may well support the weaker side in order to forestall the triumph of the potentially hegemonic state. If, however, it feels that it has no choice but to accept whatever result the conflict may produce, it is likely to consider it prudent to cultivate good relations with the powerful victor-to-be rather than with the impotent vanquished-to-be. Success in international relations, as in some other fields, leads to success; triumphant powers breed enemies, it is true, but they also breed sycophants. Statesmanship is not always heroic, but frequently finds it preferable to ride the wave of the future rather than to buck the tide.

FACTORS IN THE DECISION

Faced with a war in its international environment, a state enjoys some degree of freedom to decide upon its response. As we have indicated, it may choose to remain on the sidelines, to try to bring the war to a halt, to promote the victory of one side over the other, or to cultivate good relations with one side in anticipation of its victory. Let us now examine some of the considerations that may enter into the choice of policy.

(1) Balance of Power Calculations

Orthodox thought about international relations comes very close to taking it for granted that states will be guided by balance of power considerations in such important matters as reactions to wars. Insofar as this descriptive proposition fails, it receives a prescriptive supplement: states *should* make the balance of power their crucial concern, if they value their survival, and, realizing this, they tend to do so, almost instinctively. This has been a standard line of thought among both practicing statesmen and academic theorists. The major flaw in this consensus is that there is uncertainty and disagreement as to what it means to let balance of power considerations rule.

The academic version of balance of power theory has it that states should and normally do devote themselves to the creation and preservation of equilibrium, a situation in which every power is balanced by a roughly equal counter-power elsewhere in the system, relying upon this equipoise to provide stability for the system and safety for themselves. A corollary of this is the understanding that states should throw their weight to the weaker side in a conflict. To act in this fashion is to restore equilibrium, promoting general stability and security; to act otherwise would be to exacerbate the breakdown of equilibrium, contributing to the growth of a power too great for the survival of the system of independent states.

Literal adherence to the formal scheme elaborated by balance of power theorists is exceedingly rare. As we have noted, in the real world the leaders of states are as likely to be moved by the fear of alienating the more powerful contestant as by the hope of thwarting his victory, and they therefore choose sometimes to support the stronger rather than the weaker side. Moreover, statesmen generally treat equilibrium as a minimal rather than an optimal objective; those pressing for change must seek to acquire a margin of superiority, and even the most security-minded statesmen understandably regard a "favorable balance" as preferable to a merely "even balance." The ideal typically expressed by political leaders who espouse the balance of power is that they and their allies should be *at least* as strong as their rivals.

Hence, to say that balance of power considerations almost always figure prominently in deliberations about how a state should react to a war is not to declare that states seek equilibrium, but simply to acknowledge that their reactions are heavily influenced by concern about the effect of the war upon the international configuration of power in general and upon their own power situation in particular. Statesmen worry about the probable impact of various outcomes upon their security or their ambitions, and may be moved to take some sort of action either to halt the war or to prevent the victory of the state they consider most dangerous to themselves. That state is not necessarily the one that appears to be most powerful, for, in the real world as distinguished from academic concoctions, superiority is not equated with hostility; how another state can be expected to behave is not deemed to flow automatically from appraisal of its power.

Every war produces some change in the distribution of power in the world. States, cognizant of the fundamental importance of their standing in the distribution of power, generally find it prudent to try to anticipate, if not to determine, the nature of the change that a given war may bring about. In that sense, balance of power calculations clearly enter into the normal process of deciding what to do about other people's wars.

(2) Alliance Commitments

Closely related to balance of power calculations are concerns pertaining to alliances, which are standard parts of the mechanism of a balance of power system. By forming alliances, states undertake to improve or to stabilize their positions in the competition for power that is characteristic of the system, and the function of an alliance is to establish in advance—and usually to advertise—the position that a state will take in conflicts involving its allies. In short, alliance entails some degree of commitment to take sides, and thus would seem to have unmistakable pertinence to decisions about wars in which allies are engaged.

We would do well to broaden the notion of alliance beyond that of the formal arrangement for mutual support to include partnerships that rest upon affinity and tradition rather than upon commitment in the contractual sense. Peoples have historical friendships, cultural bonds, and sympathetic associations that often count for more than treaties. When these ties coincide with formal alliances, the expectation of mutual support is at its highest, and such bonds sometimes serve as a substitute for alliance, not necessarily inferior in effectiveness. Thus, the United States is connected with Canada and Great Britain by affinity as well as commitment, and its linkage-by-affinity with Israel is probably more meaningful than its linkage-by-commitment with, say, Turkey or Pakistan. We might add the notion of a sort of *negative* alliance, for states have historical enemies as well as friends, and in some instances appear to be as firmly set in rivalry and animosity as others appear to be in mutual understanding and cooperation. One recalls, for instance, Germany's announced expectation, during the interwar period, that most members of the League of Nations would take France's side against Germany in any clash that might arise.

This expanded notion of alliance can be summarized in the general proposition that states bring to the consideration of other people's wars a certain rigidity in their attitudes toward various other states. By reason of commitment or affinity or both, they are frequently predisposed to support some states and to oppose others.

Such predispositions are not necessarily decisive. Formal alliances are usually equipped with loopholes, and it is a rare government that has insufficient ingenuity to find or invent some plausibly respectable point of escape from a no-longer-welcome commitment to assist an ally. While having an alliance may seem sensible in ordinary times, *being* an ally in time of war is a different matter. Commitments that were designed to deter international trouble-makers may come to appear as devices for entangling the state unnecessarily in the troubles of others. Given the propensity of states to wriggle out of inconvenient commitments, an alliance is perhaps better understood as a prediction than as a guarantee. It expresses the belief of a state that in future crises it probably will find its national interests—including its interest in the international configuration of power—harmoniously linked with those of the ally; it proclaims not the willingness to sacrifice national interest for the ally but the expectation that aiding the ally will serve the state's own interest. Because that prediction may be erroneous, commitment to an ally is never wholly reliable, but the making of the commitment biases the state's policy in a crisis involving the ally. It establishes the probability of support for the ally, shifting the burden of proof to the opponent of such a policy and making it more difficult to decide otherwise.

Predispositions resting upon affinity also have limited effectiveness. Although traditional attitudes are important in the conduct of foreign policy, established friendships and enmities are notoriously mutable and special relationships are prone to fade. International relations are more likely to reflect the inconstancy of self-interestedness than the faithfulness of devotion or, for that matter, the persistence of hatred. But in the short run at least, and in the absence of compelling interest to the contrary, the sentiment of a state's population, its sense of attachment to or alienation from another state, is likely to figure significantly in the shaping of policy toward a war in which the other state is involved.

(3) Demonstration-effect Considerations

One of the factors tending to strengthen the motivation of a state to honor the promise of support that is implicit or explicit in an alliance is the belief that its performance will contribute to the shaping of its international reputation. The sense of self-interest that originally inspired the arrangement may not, in this instance, argue for involvement on the side of the ally, and the state's sense of legal obligation to honor its treaties may be negligible, but the state may be moved by the sense that other states will take note of its behavior and form conclusions about what is to be expected from it. We have here a sort of psychological domino theory that stresses the ramifications of the precedent that a state sets, or the signal that it transmits, in a particular case.

This consideration is likely to be especially prominent when a formal alliance is involved. The United States is the architect and central operator of an elaborate set of alliances, which figures as a major element in the American scheme for deterring Soviet adventurousness. Hence, the credibility of those alliances is vital to the effectiveness of the entire structure that the United States has created. One need only recall the debate about Vietnam, an important feature of which was disagreement as to whether the reputation of the United States as a responsible and reliable ally would be better served by its persisting in the defense of South Vietnam or by husbanding its resources for potential use in other sectors of the globe. The reactions of European allies were thought to be crucially important: would America's abandonment of a beleaguered ally in Southeast Asia alarm Europeans, leading them to fear the same treatment, or would it reassure them, suggesting to them that America gave priority to Europe?

Moreover, it should be remembered that an essential element of the positions held by weaker states in the international distribution of power is supplied by their alliance potential—their capacity to attract and retain the backing of states more powerful than themselves. For such states, behavior demonstrating that they take their alliances seriously is clearly mandatory.

Concern about the demonstration effect of national behavior is not limited to cases involving formal alliance. A state may be as much concerned about the consequences of breaking faith with its friends as about those of violating its treaty commitments. Americans have, from time to time, argued the importance of standing by—and being seen to stand by—leaders such as Chiang Kai-shek and the Shah of Iran. More is at stake, however, than reputation for loyalty. What sort of image does the state want to acquire in the world at large? Does it wish to give the impression of weakness, indecisiveness, or timidity? Does it wish to be regarded as ruthless and unyielding? Does it value the reputation for dependability, or prefer the advantages of unpredictability? Is it more important to be feared or to be respected for probity and fairness? Issues of this sort crowd in upon statesmen as they consider what to do about a war, knowing that the state's response to this war will in some measure affect the way in which it is generally regarded by fellow participants in the international system.

(4) Ideological Considerations

The intrusion of ideological preferences and passions into international politics is not new, as a review of the era of the French Revolution and the nineteenth-century struggle between legitimacy and republicanism would serve to remind us. The popularization of politics in our time, entailing the influence of the electronic and printed media upon mass publics in many countries throughout the world, has, however, vastly increased the role of ideological considerations in the shaping of foreign policy, including response to wars. Old-style diplomats, operating in sheltered chancelleries, may have been free to make the manipulation of power ratios their exclusive concern. Their successors have no such freedom, and they may lack such disposition; it is not self-evident that the inclination to inject ideological concerns is a monopoly of the amateurish public.

When a state begins to give attention to a war, the question of the nature of the contesting regimes is not long in arising. Which side, if either, is democratic, or socialist, or progressive, or reactionary, or Communist, or Fascist, or totalitarian? Is one side a faithful promoter of human rights? Is one a military dictatorship? Is one an agent of Islamic fundamentalism?

There is ample doctrinal support for the view that such considerations as these should be regarded as irrelevant to the conduct of foreign relations; balance of power theorists insist that concerns about relative power should dominate the making of policy, and collective security theorists urge exclusive attention to the external behavior of a state, without regard to its internal character. Moreover, international history offers evidence that ideological similarities and differences are frequently ignored; a Churchill joins with a Stalin, Islamic states fight each other, the United States supports Yugoslavia, and so forth.

The ideological factor is, however, an important element in the patterns of affinity and commitment to which we referred earlier. Ideological compatibility may rank as high as cultural similarity in the list of factors making for feelings of solidarity among states, and the formal bonds of alliance are more likely to be accepted, and to prove meaningful, within than across the lines of ideological division. While it is true that the United States was allied with the Soviet Union against Nazi Germany and has more recently been in some sense aligned with Communist China against the Soviet Union, it is improbable that the United States would ally itself with either of them against France or West Germany or India. Ideological sympathy, traditional cultural affinity, and formal alliance commitments tend to run together, although they diverge conspicuously on occasion.

Decisions about reactions to other people's wars, entailing as they do the possibility of the most serious costs that a human being can be called upon to pay, quite naturally require attention to popular attitudes toward the belligerent regimes. It is not merely a matter of asking the large impersonal question: whose victory would promote our values and strengthen the group of societies like our own? The issue literally comes home to millions of people: is that regime worthy of the sacrifice of our sons? Can we stomach fighting for that sort of government? The idea that the rulers of Saigon did not deserve to be saved by the blood of Americans was a major theme of those who opposed the American involvement in Vietnam. In a broadside issued to further his campaign for the Democratic presidential nomination in 1972, Senator George McGovern denounced American backing for the "harsh military dictatorship in South Vietnam," insisted that the United States should "cease all support of military oppressors everywhere, including Pakistan and Greece," and asserted that "We must continue to identify with and join hands with legitimate democratic governments such as Israel."[1] Similarly, Clayton Fritchey, writing in 1975 about whether the United States should become involved if a new war erupted between North and South Korea, based his negative advice entirely on an unfavorable appraisal of the domestic political morality of South Korea's right-wing dictatorship: "When the dust settles in Asia, . . . and attention is again focused on the brutal repressions of the undemocratic government . . . , Congress and the public will have to ask themselves if they want to risk another 500,000 casualties and another $150 billion in trying to salvage still another military government. . . ."[2] Fritchey wrote disapprovingly of President Ford's assertion that the United States intended to live up to its obligations; neither his nor McGovern's position assigned any weight to the legal or moral requirements of alliance or to the implications for America's position in the global power configuration of the possible conquest of a neighbor by a Communist state. Presidents of the United States are unlikely to determine policy toward other people's wars simply by subjecting the regimes involved to an ideological litmus test—perhaps the electorate, in rejecting McGovern's candidacy for that office, expressed the belief that he was too much the ideologue—but they clearly cannot ignore ideological considerations in setting that policy.

(5) Reacting to Others' Reactions

The reactions of a third party to a war may be significantly influenced by the reactions—actual, alleged, threatened, hoped for, or expected—of other bystanders. For all their vaunted sovereignty and independence, states are rarely lone wolves, intent upon going their own way heedless of the actions of other states. Wars are likely to be regarded not as isolated bits but as pieces in the elaborate jigsaw puzzle of international politics; a shrewd statesman looks at the context as well as the contest, and is as alert to the behavior of third parties as to that of the belligerents.

First of all, states take into account what other states are doing or appear to be planning to do. The United States, for instance, is very likely to ask what the Soviet Union is doing. Is it giving support, directly or indirectly, overtly or covertly, to one of the parties? In the case of a civil war, has the Soviet Union intervened in some fashion? Has the Soviet Union so clearly chosen a side that the victory of that side will constitute a triumph for the Soviets? If that is believed to be true, the argument might be raised that the United States should intervene on the other side, undertaking to thwart the Soviet design. Alternatively, it might be argued that the United States should abstain, lest it precipitate a dangerous showdown with the Soviet Union. In any event, what the United States decides to do or not to do about a war is likely to be influenced by what the Soviet Unon is perceived as doing.

The United States, of course, responds to the policy of many states, not just that of the Soviet Union; in some sense, all states react to the behavior of all the others. In this era of institutionalized multilateralism, there is a considerable tendency for states to follow the crowd, to go along with the majority or at least to avoid falling conspicuously out of line with the dominant diplomatic reaction to such events as wars. International organizations both mobilize majorities that attract, and designate pariahs that repel, conformist states. For many states, not being on the same side of a conflict as Israel is mandatory, and both the Soviet Union and the United States serve as poles of repulsion for what might be called their negative clienteles. The object of the most widespread and determined shunning today is South Africa, whose partnership most states would find a cause of ideological discomfort. For instance, one source of the opposition that halted American involvement in the struggle over the political direction of Angola in 1976 was the conviction that the United States could not afford to be seen as collaborating with South Africa. As this suggests, reaction to the positions taken by other states is in some measure a function of their ideological identification.

Secondly, states take into account how other states are likely to react to what they may do. An important aspect of policy-making is the predicting of the consequences, in the behavior of other states, of a proposed line of action. If we intervene on one side, will that induce our allies to do so as well, or suggest to them that they need not do so? Will it provoke our rivals to intervene on the other side? If we remain aloof, will we thereby encourage other states to do the same and thus contribute to localization of the conflict? Or will our rivals take advantage of our abstention to move in and take control of the situation? Answers to questions of this sort can seldom be certain, and much of the debate about foreign policy in such a society as the United States turns on honest disagreement about the implications of proposed lines of action or inaction not only for the immediate situations with which they purport to deal—other people's wars, for instance—but also for the behavior of other states. What the United States decides to do about a war is clearly of especial importance—not simply for the United States, and for the parties to the conflict, but for the entire world. The American reaction to a war may be the decisive element in determining whether it will remain limited or ignite a global conflagration. Whether the happier of those results is more likely to be promoted by American abstention or by American involvement is the question for debate, and the answers put forward will depend in large measure on estimates as to the responses of other states to the policy adopted by the United States.

(6) Collective Security Principles

The calamity of World War I stimulated the elaborate development of a rather simple theoretical scheme for bringing order to international relations: the idea of a collective security system. According to this doctrine, the states of the world should constitute an organization dedicated to deterring or, if necessary, defeating the attempt by any state to achieve change by military action—dedicated, that is, to enforcing the rule that the only acceptable use of force in international relations is to thwart aggression. To this end, states would be firmly and clearly committed to participate in joint action, including military action if it should be required, to defend any member of the system against improper attack. Ideally, under such an arrangement every state would be, and would be aware that it was, debarred from reaching its international goals by military force, and every state would be, and would know that it was, protected against coercion by more powerful states. No state would be strong enough to succeed in aggressive action, and every state would be strong enough to succeed in defensive action. By putting the strength of all at the disposal of each, for defensive purposes only, the scheme would in effect equalize the security of all states.

This theoretical scheme provides a uniform and unequivocal answer to the question of how a state should respond to other people's wars. It should act without reference to the belligerents' identity, size, power, geographical location, strategic importance, record of behavior, presumed policy intentions for the future, or ideological complexion. It should choose between the contestants solely on the basis of the rightfulness of their resort to violence—opposing the one that is guilty of attempting by military means to achieve an objective, and defending the one that is innocent of such behavior and is using force only to resist the achievement of change through violence. The decision to support the party resisting aggression should be made promptly, contributing to the predictability of the system's effective operation. This is to say that the decision *in principle*—the commitment to the propositions that the state's vital interest requires the suppression of violent disturbance of international order and that the state should therefore resolutely take part in collective efforts to control violence—should have been made well in advance, when the state accepted membership in the organized system. Having accepted the essential elements of collective security doctrine and assumed the obligations of membership in a collective security system, the state has only to ascertain the pertinent facts of a concrete case: which side is engaged in aggression, and which in defense? Policy has been set in advance; all that remains is its application to the case at hand.

The intention to establish a collective security system figured prominently in the creation of both the League of Nations and the United Nations, but it is doubtful that any state has ever genuinely committed itself to the obligations of collective security, in the sense of approaching every instance of armed conflict with the pre-established resolution to support whichever party may be found to be resisting aggression. No state has taken the view that what it should do about a war is always a foregone conclusion; uncertainties and disagreements persist and make decisions about such matters difficult. The facile application of the collective security formula simply does not occur.

For many reasons, the anti-aggression consideration put forward by collective security theory has limited appeal. The idea of a collective security system is enormously attractive so long as one focuses entirely on its promised results; the world finds it easy to endorse collective security, defined as stable order for all to enjoy. That idea loses its attraction when one focuses on the dangerous and costly duties that it requires states to undertake; the world has grave reservations about collective security, defined as weighty responsibility for all to bear. When a state is confronted with other people's wars, it may have second thoughts about the proposition that they are, in fact, its own wars. Doing what collective security doctrine says it must do about them may not appear wise, proper, or even feasible. Moreover, as we have noted, numerous other considerations compete with the anti-aggression theme as determinants of policy.

While collective security theory has not transformed international relations in the systematic way contemplated by its champions, it has made its imprint on the thinking about foreign policy of many influential people. Its theme that anybody's war is everybody's war, because small rents in the fabric of world order may lead to ghastly rips, enjoys considerable currency. American reaction to wars in all parts of the world, for instance, frequently entails pondering on their potential consequences for the world in general and the United States in particular. The central doctrine of collective security, that aggression is intolerable and that states ought, in their own interest as well as in fulfillment of their international responsibility, to contribute to its defeat, can be identified as an element in the reactions of many states, including the United States, to many of the armed conflicts with which they are confronted. The difficulty of applying this doctrine is indicated by the numerous cases in which there is sharp disagreement, within as well as among states, as to which belligerent is the aggressor. The weakness of states' commitment to the anti-aggression formula is evidenced by their tendency to limit their opposition to declarations and votes for multilateral resolutions of condemnation; rhetoric is the compromise between the equally unacceptable extremes of abandonment and enforcement of the rule against aggression. These reservations aside, it is clear that in the United States and many other countries any debate about how to react to a war is virtually certain to include argument as to whether one side or the other is guilty of aggression and as to the relative propriety and prudence of tolerating or helping to counter aggression.

(7) Just Cause Considerations

From the point of view of pacifists and quasi-pacifists, collective security doctrine has always been suspect because it accords legitimacy to—and even proposes mandatory participation in—wars to defeat aggression. Since ingenious aggressors can usually fabricate plausible claims to be engaging in defensive action, this doctrine may be exploited so as to make it confer its blessing far too generously. Pacifists are inclined to consider collective security a scheme for making war, not for preventing it.

In today's world, however, the chief objection to collective security is that it licenses wars too stingily, not too generously. It limits acceptable war to defense, in effect insisting that military force must never be used to press for the alteration of the status quo. Collective security theory revives, but drastically circumscribes, traditional just war doctrine. The latter suits the mood of our time far better; in this era of revolutionary challenge to the European-style international system, the notion that it is just to fight to achieve justice will not be put down by the argument that victims of injustice must achieve change peacefully or not at all. In truth, not many human beings really believe that war to remedy injustice is in all circumstances reprehensible. When we think of the horrors of war, we may endorse collective security's insistence that no political objective can justify resort to violence. When we think of the horror of established injustice, we are inclined to forget that endorsement.

Hence, the question, "who has committed aggression?", tends to be supplanted by the question, "who is fighting to establish or perpetuate injustice?". The evaluation of the merits of the causes for which the parties to a conflict are deemed to be fighting is clearly a major part of the process by which third parties determine their responses to war. The decision to exert pressure upon the parties to cease fire, or to assist one or the other in achieving victory, may be strongly influenced by sympathy or antipathy for such purposes as ending colonialism, undermining military dictatorships, spreading Communism, achieving Palestinian self-determination, extirpating apartheid, strengthening the forces of democracy, or guaranteeing Israel's right to a secure existence. When the values of peace and justice appear to conflict, the former is not always preferred to the latter.

(8) Just Means Considerations

The effort to limit the means and methods of warfare and thereby to confine the damage wrought by war has always inspired controversy as to both its feasibility and its desirability. Mankind seems to have concluded, however, that meagre success is better than none; the danger of making war more palatable by making it less destructive ultimately seems less impressive than the catastrophe that one can envision if no effort is made to regulate the conduct of war.

Hence, reactions to real or alleged infractions of formal rules or informal understandings about the conduct of war often figure prominently in the policy decisions of bystanding and onlooking states. Atrocity stories, allegations of gratuitous brutality, and charges of the use of forbidden weapons are exploited by belligerents, in the knowledge that the leanings of third parties may be affected as much by perceptions of the rightness of the manner in which the conflict is waged as by judgment of the cause for which it is waged. Germany's resort to unrestricted submarine warfare clearly had something to do with the entry of the United States into World War I. America's use of napalm evidently contributed to the unpopularity of its involvement in Vietnam. The introduction of thermonuclear weapons into a war, particularly against a non-nuclear state, is inhibited by the virtual certainty that it would be politically disastrous. Rough and tough though the game of power politics may be, the image of the unscrupulous and inhumane Big Bully is not one that states engaged in war, concerned about the reactions of third parties, normally think it advisable to cultivate. Considerations of decency, fairness, and moderation—anomalous as they may seem to those who conceive war simply as hell—may be an important factor in what states do about other people's wars.

(9) Practical Considerations

"What should we do?" ultimately turns on the answer to the question, "What *can* we do?". States obviously vary greatly in their capacity to affect the general run of wars, but the capacity of a given state to have an impact upon a given war may be quite unrelated to its general standing in the global system. One of the most serious responsibilities of the political, diplomatic, and military leaders of states is to assess the possibilities and limits of action related to wars, undertaking to subject preferences and choices dictated by sense of obligation to the discipline of feasibility.

In matters of assistance to a state involved in war, the "for whom" question is no less important than the "by whom" question. "Helpability," the capacity of a state or regime to put assistance to effective use, is a consideration that other states ignore at their peril. In the Vietnam case, the argument that Saigon *could* not be saved entered into the controversy about American intervention along with the view that it *should* not be saved, and one of the lessons frequently drawn from that unhappy experience is that the United States should take greater care to avoid committing itself to causes that are doomed from the outset.

Failure is not, however, the worst possible result of an intrusion of some sort into a war. The danger of counterproductiveness, of bringing about the opposite of what one intends, is always present. Would our support of our favorite stimulate the granting of decisive assistance to the other side? Can we influence the outcome of this war without getting ourselves engaged in a conflict that we cannot afford? Would our involvement limit and shorten the war—or expand and prolong it? Can we be sure that a proposed course of action on our part would tend to prevent rather than to promote the conflict's precipitating World War III? Questions of this kind cannot be excluded from deliberations about reactions to war.

(10) Domestic Political Considerations

What a state decides to do or not to do in the international arena is affected by, and has an effect upon, its domestic political life. This is true in some measure of all states, and particularly of such a democratic society as the United States. From Washington's Farewell Address to that of Lyndon Johnson, evidence has accumulated that calculations of the domestic consequences of alternative policies in reaction to other people's wars are an indispensable part of the policymaking process. Sometimes the government of an open and pluralistic society risks adverse reaction if it fails to exert its influence over a conflict, while at other times it courts disaster if it becomes actively involved. Thus, in dealing with the situation in El Salvador the United States government must maneuver between the slogans, "No more Cubas" and "No more Vietnams." The nature of domestic criticism tends to fluctuate with the passage of time. In the short term, it is usually safer for a government to stand aside than to act; the accusation of imprudence in failing to intervene in an armed conflict normally comes after the event. As Neville Chamberlain could testify, what seemed initially "peace in our time" became, retrospectively, appeasement in the opprobrious sense.

The proper task of a government in shaping foreign policy is not simply to cater to demonstrated or anticipated popular moods. A government owes it to its constituency to do what needs to be done, trusting that in the long run such behavior will command the society's approval.

Political courage consists in refusing to take domestic political repercussions as absolutely decisive in whatever case may be at hand. In the broader picture, however, defiance of passionately held popular convictions about how the state should perform in relation to other people's wars is reduced to foolhardiness. Ultimately, what a state *can* do is a function of what its people are willing to do, so that taking domestic political considerations into account is a matter not so much of choosing to be democratic as of realistically facing up to necessity.

CONCLUSION

The relative importance of the various considerations that we have identified as entering into decisions pertaining to other people's wars varies from state to state and from time to time. Indeed, it varies from case to case, so that neither the consistent application of a pattern by a state nor even the consistent advocacy of a pattern by a faction within a state is likely to be found. Theorists of balance of power and of collective security have set forth formulas that are advised for general application. While both have been praised by scholars and statesmen, neither has in fact been accepted as the source of ready answers to the question, "What should we do about other people's wars?". As the twentieth century moves on toward its conclusion, the clearest feature of the situation is the rejection by states of doctrinal determinants of decision and their insistent reliance upon pragmatic calculations, case by case.

In the United States, reactions to wars are marked today by confusion, uncertainty, and conflict of attitudes. Whether one believes that Vietnam destroyed a pre-existing consensus or revealed the illusory quality of that consensus, it is evident that the struggle over American involvement in that conflict introduced a period marked by the absence of consensus as to what considerations ought to govern American reactions to wars. This situation should be acknowledged as dashing, for the foreseeable future, any hope that the United Nations might somehow mobilize a multilateral response to disturbances of international order, in the manner of a collective security system; if Americans cannot agree among themselves as to what factors should determine the policy of the United States toward wars between other states, what chance is there for agreement on this matter among the members of the enormously heterogeneous global system?

For better or for worse, neither predictability nor uniformity of reaction to other people's wars is to be expected. The issue of what to do about such wars will be taken seriously by states. Precisely because of its seriousness, states will insist upon dealing with it pragmatically, developing what they hope will prove to be the appropriate combination of considerations for determining their reactions in each case as it arises.

PART THREE

The Rejection of Collective Security

The doctrine of collective security is a prescription for an institutionalized arrangement to maintain the security of all members of a system of states by guaranteeing that an attack by any member against another will engender the combined resistance of all the others whose contribution to the common defense may be needed. This idea first attracted general attention during World War I, as Allied statesmen considered the problem of reconstructing the international system so as to obviate the recurrence of that sort of catastrophe. Ever since that time, it has figured prominently in both diplomatic and academic discussions of international relations. It has, from time to time, aroused devoted advocacy and enthusiastic support. President Woodrow Wilson described it as "the basis, the only conceivable basis, for the future peace of the world," and Gilbert Murray viewed it as "the obvious way to prevent war."[1] The general international organizations established after both the global wars of the twentieth century were conceived, in part, as experiments in the formation of a collective security system.

Notwithstanding the lip service that the project of setting up a collective security system recurrently enjoys, my thesis is that the idea has in fact been almost universally and quite definitively rejected. It should be obvious that under the auspices neither of the League of Nations nor of the United Nations has the world created or operated a systematic arrangement for collective action to protect any and all potential victims of aggression by deterring all would-be aggressors or defeating all actual aggressors. Gilbert Murray attributed the outbreak of World War II to "the betrayal, or at least the nonfulfillment, of the pledges of the great European nations" to apply the collective security formula. "That was," he wrote, "the hardest duty which members of the League undertook; it was indispensable; and they failed in it. Had they been ready to act in time, there would have been no talk of force: had they been ready to use force, there would have been no need for it. It was because the aggressor could always count on the Great Powers not being ready to face a risk of war that he felt free to do his worst against smaller victims."[2] Indeed, one might argue that the European leaders had never really accepted the collective security obligation. They ratified the Covenant of the League, but they defected from its provisions for joint action against aggression just as surely as did the United States, albeit less openly and honestly. What came later were the revelation and the acknowledgment of the European rejection of collective security.

Murray's complaint, written in 1939, was echoed in 1981 by an American spokesman at the General Assembly of the United Nations, Eugene V. Rostow, who asserted that "The last two decades have witnessed a rising tide of threats to the peace, breaches of the peace, and aggressions" in violation of Article 2 (4) of the Charter of the United Nations, noted that "As the fever of aggression spreads, the world community does less and less to vindicate the basic principle" contained in that Charter provision, and warned that, unless the world acts to uphold that principle, "the slide toward anarchy will engulf us all."[3]

Murray and Rostow, speaking a generation apart, said substantially the same thing: not that collective security has failed, but that it has been rejected, dropped, abandoned, betrayed. Humanity has had a sort of love-hate affair with the idea of collective security since World War I. Most people who think about international relations have favored a collective security system when they have thought about the peaceful order that it promises to ensure, but they have opposed it when they have thought about the obligations that it imposes upon member states; they have been attracted by the prospective results and repelled by the prescribed method.

There is simply no evidence that, if the Soviet Union should attack Poland, all the world would rally to Poland's defense. The leaders of Israel, or Nicaragua, or El Salvador, or Angola, or South Africa would not be justified in relaxing, confidently expecting that the United Nations would mobilize collective force to defend their countries against aggression. It is not to be taken for granted that the United States will intervene, by armed force if necessary, whenever any state, anywhere in the world, requires protection against aggressive attack by some other state—or that the American people would support or even tolerate such a policy. For many, the rejection of collective security has been at most half-conscious; not all who have abandoned the concept have confessed, even to themselves, that they have in fact repudiated it. Nonetheless, I am convinced that this approach to the maintenance of peace, so logical and plausible that many have regarded it as the *obvious* solution to the problem of world order, has never had a great deal of genuine support and must now be described as having been flatly rejected both by the leaders who act on behalf of states and by the peoples who constitute states.

The reasons for the rejection of collective security are many, and I shall not repeat the criticisms of that doctrine developed by students of international relations, including myself, over the years.[4] Rather than attempting a comprehensive, or even a balanced, analysis, I should like to concentrate on a few of the factors that seem to me not to have been given adequate attention by those of us who have tried to understand and explain the rejection of collective security.

WHY HAS COLLECTIVE SECURITY BEEN REJECTED?

A large part of the opposition to collective security has always derived from skepticism about its effectiveness, from the sense that it has failed or that it cannot be made to work reliably in the real world for which it is prescribed. Much of this criticism is valid, and some who reject collective security must be credited with having done so because of a realistic understanding of its shortcomings. From Woodrow Wilson in 1919 to Gilbert Murray in 1939, the champions of collective security were overly sanguine about the adequacy of their scheme for saving the world. I pass over denial of its feasibility, however, to concentrate on other things. I also pass over the objection that emphasizes the unwillingness of states to respect the prohibition of aggression, the argument that the members of a multistate system inevitably engage in aggressive behavior. That may well be true; at least the tendency toward aggression is inherent in the situation if not in the nature of the units of a multistate system, and the phenomenon of aggression is a persistent part of international reality. But this confirms, rather than contradicts, the theory of collective security, which assumes the incidence of international aggression and undertakes to cope with it. The fact of aggression may be taken to prove not that collective security is impossible but that it is necessary, just as crime serves to confirm the need for, rather than to deny the feasibility of, domestic systems of law and order. The central objection to collective security has not been that it prohibits states from committing aggression, but that it requires them to become involved in inhibiting or resisting aggression. The troublesome aspect of Article 10 of the Covenant of the League of Nations was the commitment to preserve, rather than the commitment to respect, the territorial integrity and political independence of other states. The reaction against collective security stems not from states' denial of the duty to obey the law against aggression but from their rejection of the duty to uphold that law; it is not that states insist upon being criminals, but that they balk at being policemen.

The heart of the collective security idea is that states will maintain international order by proclaiming and proving their determination to act cooperatively against any violator of that order. Therein lies the trouble that accounts in large measure for the rejection of collective security. To paraphrase what someone has said about Christianity, it is not that collective security has been tried and found wanting, but that it has been found difficult and not tried. I see the rejection of collective security primarily as an expression of the reluctance of states to take part in enforcement measures (sanctions, to use the conventional academic term)—and, in this context, I intend the word, state, to refer to virtually all the people in that political unit, from prime ministers to peasants. Why have the world's governments and peoples, leaders and followers, shied away from the job that collective security theory assigns to them, that of deterring or defeating any and all aggressors who might challenge the order of the international system?

We should note that enthusiasm for collective security—that is, declared willingness to undertake the enforcement duties that membership in such a system entails—seems to appear among the participants in a coalition that is in process of winning, or has just won, a major war. It is a product of the afterglow of successful war. It is equally noteworthy that this enthusiasm seems to disappear after a few years, when the afterglow of war fades into mere aftermath, and a postwar period begins. This pattern of waxing and waning of support for collective security can be observed in connection with both World War I and World War II, and to a lesser degree with the Korean War. The thesis that collective security is the wartime ideology of a victorious coalition, with its implication that commitment to collective security cannot survive the rigors of peacetime, seems both to fit the facts and to sum up a number of the factors that help to explain the rejection of the doctrine. In short, we may find that the rejection of collective security is to a considerable degree simply a function of the evaporation of the wartime mood.

The casualties of peace include the sense of simplicity and clarity that prevails during war. I think it was Dr. Johnson who said that nothing concentrates the mind like the prospect of a hanging; we might suggest that nothing clears the national head like involvement in the achievement of a smashing military triumph. During the war, the case for collective security seems unassailable and the scheme seems neat and logical. The wartime allies see no difficulty about defining aggression and identifying the aggressor; the aggressor, whose guilt is obvious, is the enemy, and the existence of the winning coalition proves that right-minded governments can recognize aggressors when they see them. The lines are clearly drawn between the Good Guys and the Bad Guys, and the moral self-confidence of the coalition is not greatly disturbed by qualms about doing whatever may be necessary, however repugnant the means may be in themselves, to win the war. The priorities are clear: defeat the enemy, and then turn to the shaping of a new and better world. What is this foolishness about possible collision between perceptions of national interest and the obligations of a collective security system? We are collaborating to defeat a challenge to the order upon which we all depend, we find it very much in our national interest to do so, and we find it impossible to imagine that decent and sensible people in the future will fail to recognize that they have a vital interest in collaborating to keep the peace so that they will not be obliged, as we have been, to collaborate to win a terrible war!

Such is the mood that generates collective security schemes. For better or for worse—and it is clearly worse for collective security—it is not sustainable in peacetime. Simplicity gives way to complexity, clarity to ambiguity, certainty to perplexity, self-confidence to self-doubt, consensus to argument, and solidarity to disunity. This is what causes people, guiltily but nonetheless genuinely, to look back at some wartime periods with nostalgia: those were the days when we had a sense of national purpose, when we all pulled together, and when we knew what it was to feel loyal—and loyalty was regarded as honorable! As war recedes into the background, all the great "of courses" that sustain collective security vanish: of course we agree that no cause justifies resort to aggression; of course we have a vital interest in suppressing aggression wherever and whenever it may occur; of course we can spot the aggressor and agree on joint action against him. When the artificial light generated by war is extinguished, we find it difficult to understand how decent and sensible people could have imagined that aggression would be clear-cut and aggressors conspicuous, that third states would invariably regard aggression as unjustified and as damaging to their own interests, and that the organized international system would find it possible to adopt and carry out a collective reaction to every act of aggression.

Quasi-Pacifism

A major factor in the rejection of collective security is what I shall call *quasi-pacifism*. Full-fledged, unqualified pacifism would be a major factor, except that it is so rare; indeed, most people who think that they are absolute pacifists are, in fact, quasi-pacifists. By quasi-pacifism, I mean something less than the absolute refusal to participate in war but a very strong aversion to war, a general disposition to believe that involvement in war is wrong and foolish and unnecessary and counterproductive, an anti-military bias, and—to sum it all up—a decided preference for the *soft* rather than the *hard* line in international affairs.

This means, of course, that quasi-pacifism is an obstacle to the sincere acceptance of either the balance of power or the collective security prescription for state behavior. For all the differences that are emphasized (and often exaggerated) between these two approaches, balance of power and collective security are fundamentally alike in that both of them rely ultimately upon the threat or the use of force to control disturbers of the international peace; they are *hard*, not *soft*, approaches to order. They define the problem of keeping order rather differently—balance of power thought stresses controlling aggrandizement, while collective security theory focuses on controlling aggression—but they both propose to deal with the problem by means that offend the quasi-pacifist. Moreover, both of them place a premium upon committedness and the resultant predictability of state behavior. Though they prescribe different formulas, they are at one in urging states to act in international affairs according to formula. This is to say that balance of power and collective security stand in joint opposition to the policy of keeping one's distance from international conflicts or of playing the unpredictable role of the auxiliary power; both of them provide a rationale for states' being committed to, and resolutely intent upon, engagement in coercive measures whenever they may be required for the maintenance of world order. When Wilson urged Europeans to shift from the balance of power to the collective security approach, he was asking that they become more, not less, committed to the use of military might for order-keeping purposes, for his scheme required them to substitute alliance with any and every state that should become the victim of aggression for the more selective and restricted alliance commitments of the balance of power system. Collective security, in short, imposes heavier military responsibilities upon states than does balance of power; the latter is a half-way house to the former. That being so, it is not surprising that European states should have balked at moving from a balance of power to a collective security system. Nor is it surprising that Americans have at most reached the nearer of those destinations, tentatively accepting alliance with some but recoiling at the thought of being committed to the protection of all.

Collective security is ultimately a scheme for military deterrence or military defense on a universal scale. Softliners, or quasi-pacifists, quite naturally have always opposed it. William Jennings Bryan put the quasi-pacifistic case against collective security very effectively in debates with William Howard Taft, representing the League to Enforce Peace, during World War I.[5] More to the point is the fact that whole societies drift into quasi-pacifism once they put their wars behind them, and find the obligations of a collective security system less and less congenial as the war that stimulated construction of the system fades from memory. It is perhaps more accurate to say that twentieth-century Western societies are fundamentally quasi-pacifistic (or debellicized, to use the terminology of Michael Howard), and that the hardness of approach that makes them play with the idea of collective security is a wartime aberration, an artificial and ephemeral mood. The return to normality is the resumption of the soft, anti-military approach to international relations.

Ambivalence about the hard approach to international order has been endemic in the collective security movement from its beginning. Take the case of G. Lowes Dickinson, a leading British figure in the formulation of the collective security idea and an influential advocate of the League of Nations. In his book, *Causes of International War*, first published in 1920, Dickinson dogmatically asserted that professional military officers find war congenial to their interests and ideals. He wrote that "if a man has trained himself for war, he must . . . desire to put his training into practice," and that "to maintain an officer class is to maintain a class of men who cannot work against war, and must work for it, unless they undergo a conversion that would shatter their whole life."[6] Moreover, he described the state as "armed egotism," held that "the essence of the activity of states is the pursuit of power by

The reply was even more extraordinary than the question. A reputedly hawkish member of a new Administration committed to increased strength, vigilance, and toughness in foreign affairs, a regime regarded by its critics at home and abroad as excessively bellicose, purported to be uncertain as to the capacity of the United States to sustain a foreign policy that might entail the cost of even a single military casualty. He did not respond to the question, as one might have expected, by reminding the television audience that the United States is a superpower, bearing the responsibilities of global leadership, and asserting that the recent election of President Reagan proved that the American people were prepared to support a more forceful performance in world affairs. He did speak in that vein later in the program, emphasizing the importance of communicating to the Soviet Union the fact that America had abandoned weakness and irresoluteness for strength and firmness. His response to that earlier question did not, however, contribute to the conveyance of such a message. When the minister in charge of one of the world's greatest military establishments expresses the plaintive hope that his government's policy will not be disrupted by the people's fear that a single casualty might presage massive losses, one is less impressed by the bellicosity of the regime than by the quasi-pacifism of the country over which it presides.

I do not intend to suggest that extreme caution about involvement in armed conflict is unwise or improper. Trigger-happiness is not preferable to gun-shyness. Indeed, sound policy requires sober consideration of what should and can be done, uninhibited by doctrinaire dispositions either to resort, or not to resort, to military action. What the Weinberger interview tells us is that the present-day American approach to international relations is considerably softer in concrete action than in abstract declaration, and that the truly ridiculous question would be whether the United States might be willing to participate in a collective security system. The mood of quasi-pacifism is not uniformly spread over the world, but it is sufficiently strong in a sufficient number of states to rank as a major factor in the rejection of collective security.

Lack of Moral Self-Confidence

Another factor, closely related to quasi-pacifism, that has contributed to the rejection of collective security is the decline of moral self-confidence in the West. All defense policy, from the unilateral to the universal, depends heavily upon the conviction that one has something that deserves to be defended. For most people, the issue of the moral propriety of military defense cannot be dissociated from the issue of the moral worthiness of that which is to be defended. The answer to the question, "Is the stability of the international system worth defending?", is crucial to the prospects for collective security.

In this respect—and despite his anti-militarism, which bent him toward quasi-pacifism—Gilbert Murray was the ideal champion of collective security. His volume of essays, *From the League to U.N.*, contains a remarkable paean to Western Civilization. Murray, a distinguished classical scholar at Oxford, deeply believed in the infinite value of the Western heritage; he saw it as a treasure to which all men are heirs and to the preservation of which all should be devoted. He indignantly denied that war was a symptom of a corrupt civilization, insisting instead that it be regarded as a barbarous threat to the most precious product of human history.[10] One could almost say that Murray was a collective security theorist and advocate because he was a classicist; he wanted to rally mankind to the defense of the values that he loved. Writing in the thirties, when the commitment of members of the League of Nations to the idea of collective security was being revealed as hollow pretense, he became deeply pessimistic as he was forced to question whether his fellow-men thought those values worth defending. He wrote: "I believe no social order ever failed unless it had lost confidence in its vitality, its value to human beings, and its right to live."[11]

A case can be made that the decline of that confidence is responsible, in large part, for the rejection of collective security. If a collective security system were in existence today, most of the non-Western world would regard it not as an arrangement for the defense of civilization but as a scheme for the perpetuation of an unjust status quo, marked by the ruthless hegemony of the West—and many in the West would either echo the accusation or acquiesce in it. For our purposes, what is important is not the question of the validity of the charge but the fact that it is widely accepted. The international system is not generally considered to be sufficiently just, or sufficiently open to the achievement of justice, to deserve the kind of protection that a collective security scheme would undertake to give it. The world, including much of the West, is more inclined to approve than to oppose aggression when it appears to serve a cause that the Third World characterizes as just. The United Nations, along with many other international organizations, confers legitimacy upon coercive efforts to alter established international arrangements in pursuit of anticolonial and related objectives. The defense of order against assaults by outraged protestors of injustice requires either less moral sensitivity or more moral conviction than most beneficiaries of the international status quo possess.

Uncertainty about the moral quality of the established order that one may be called upon to defend in a system of collective security is complicated by the fact that the instrument upon which such a system ultimately relies for the defense of order is the same as that which disrupts order: military force. The distinction between aggression and resistance to aggression does not lie in the eye of the beholder, but in the minds and wills of the antagonists; the proper characterization of the behavior of the opposing parties turns not upon what they do, but upon why they do it. The claim to be resisting aggression is notoriously subject to abuse, and is almost invariably challenged. Participants in collective security systems need thick skins and a great deal of moral self-confidence—more than they are likely to have—if they are to avoid being shaken by the charge that their resort to arms is as reprehensible as that to which they are responding. Morally sensitive members of the international system tend to have much the same sort of difficulty with collective security that morally sensitive citizens of the state often have with capital punishment.

Americans in particular, and especially since the debacle of Vietnam, are lacking in assurance as to the worthiness of such purportedly order-keeping ventures as their government might undertake. The suspicion that their country is somehow irremediably biased in favor of perpetuating oppressive regimes and saving the skins of military dictators has caused some Americans to develop what might be called a theory of anticipatory unjust war—the notion that whatever cause the United States chooses to support by military action is automatically suspect, a kind of national paraphrase of Groucho Marx's contempt for any club that would grant him membership. More broadly, the West is beset by feelings of guilt. Moral self-confidence today is almost exclusively the property of those who are dedicated to changing the world, by force if necessary. It is therefore not available to support a system of collective security—which is, after all, a scheme for resisting the violent approach to change.

Lack of International Civic Virtue

The last factor in the rejection of collective security that I should like to consider is the lack of what we might call international civic virtue, or a sense of international public responsibility. The dismal story of the 1930s has often been told—how the major democracies failed to stand up to the aggressors, thereby bringing the world to disaster. Writing about the surrender of the League powers to Mussolini in the Abyssinian case, Murray commented that: "Our civilization had announced to the world and to history that it had not the necessary sense of corporate duty, not the necessary strength of mind, to defend itself." What was fatally lacking, according to him, was "enough civil courage and sense of public duty to make the law-abiding nations combine in defence of the law."[12] Theorists of collective security have always held that their system requires governments and peoples not to renounce their national interests in favor of some higher loyalty but to understand that their most vital national interest is the maintenance of a stable international order. Collective security doctrine thus insists that effective concern for the national welfare must be community-centered, that only in devotion to the peace and order of the whole can any part find safety. In short, a successful system of collective security presumes that its members will share a sense of responsibility for the defense of the entire collectivity; nothing less than that can motivate them to the faithful performance of the dangerous and potentially costly duties that the system imposes upon them. That essential spirit is not frequently in evidence.

The standard explanation of this crucial deficiency emphasizes the invincible, incorrigible selfishness of the state. In regard to community spirit, the international system is compared unfavorably with the national society. Domestically, it is said, we are animated by a common loyalty and concern for the general welfare, in contrast to the ruthless, every-state-for-itself spirit of the international system. Gilbert Murray quotes the British Foreign Minister, Sir John Simon, as having said in defense of his government's failure to oppose Japan in the Manchurian crisis: "The object of my policy is to keep my own country out of trouble."[13] Within the state, nationalism typically makes for solidarity and sovereignty stands for central control and deference to authority. By contrast, in the international system, nationalism dramatizes division and sovereignty is associated with anarchy. In international relations, to say that a state pursues its national interest is all too often to say that it acts selfishly, and to say that it is sovereign is to say that it claims, and is acknowledged to have, the *right* to act selfishly—that is, without regard for the interest of the society of which it is a part. How then could one expect a society composed of sovereign national states to operate a collective security system?

When this analysis moves down from the abstract entity called the state to the human level of government and people, or leaders and followers, the situation seems more palatable—but not more conducive to the genuine acceptance of collective security. Governments, we are told, are the trustees of their societies, agents responsible for safeguarding the interests of the peoples over whom they rule. For them to pursue the international common interest in preference to the national interest would be to betray their trust; when Sir John Simon let an aggressor sin with impunity because he wanted to keep Great Britain out of trouble, he may have offended Gilbert Murray but he honored his moral obligation as a member of the British government. Murray adds to this an argument based on the theory of representation. Leaving moral responsibility aside and assuming simply that representatives are in the business of nursing their constituencies, he argues that there can be no devotion to the community of mankind until there are political leaders responsive to global constituencies. As things stand, no one in a position of power has either a moral responsibility that permits him, or a political interest that requires him, to subordinate national advantage to international stability.[14] As for ordinary people, they give their allegiance to the state, and their loyalty is effectively circumscribed by its boundaries. Hence, civic virtue in the real world is a national, not an international, phenomenon. Neither leaders nor followers can be expected to exhibit the sense of global responsibility that must underlie any genuine acceptance of collective security.

I have some difficulty with this analysis, on the ground that it paints not too somber a picture of the international system but too rosy a picture of the domestic scene. Civic virtue is in short supply at every level; if the international system attracted as much of this commodity as, say, the United States, I am not sure that the prospects for a collective security system would be greatly improved. Large numbers of young American men have in recent years ignored the legal requirement of registration for a currently non-existent military draft, and it seems clear that any proposal for a draft, let alone for universal national service, would encounter insurmountable political difficulties. After all, Ronald Reagan, not the least patriotic of American leaders, argued as a presidential candidate in 1980 that the government has no proper claim to the mandatory service of young people except in the most severe national emergencies. Note the following newspaper report:

> Emotions run high among people resisting draft registration. Forms have been burned outside post offices, rallies have been held at colleges and threats have been made to public personalities who support draft registration.

> "There is a lot of anger . . . because these kids feel the draft is irrelevant, an imposition in their lives they don't comprehend," says Dr. Steven Pieczinik, a psychiatrist in Washington who studied draft evasion during the Vietnam war. "The kids today don't want to get into anything they feel is irrelevant to their career lives. The concepts of ideology and loyalty are very foreign to them, and they don't understand why they have to spend two years of their lives where they might get killed for something that has no meaning to them."[15]

It appears that enthusiasm within the United States for serving the nation is not overwhelmingly greater than for serving the world. Moreover, the international system and the state are not engaged in a zero-sum game in this regard. They do not compete for shares of a finite quantity of civic virtue, so that the more the state attracts, the less remains for the larger system. On the contrary, an increase in the devotion of Americans to national service would be likely to strengthen the prospects for American service to international security undertakings.

National societies operate and survive with relatively little civic virtue of an active sort, because they can rely instead upon the use of mercenaries. This was brought home to me several years ago, when I noticed that the trash collectors had spilled garbage in the parking area outside my apartment house in Jerusalem. I deplored it, reflected that the garbage might rapidly become a health hazard in Israel's climate, and, of course, passed on. Returning a few minutes later, I found that the mess had been cleared away. Assuming that one of my neighbors had done the job, I felt guilty and remarked to myself, admiringly, that Israelis have more civic virtue than Americans—perhaps because of their society's perpetually beleaguered situation. Unfortunately, I later learned that a municipal crew had cleaned up the clutter; how many Israelis passed by on the other side, as I did, before the bureaucratic Good Samaritan did the job, I shall never know.

This is a true story, but it is a parable, too. Modern man is accustomed to having someone else do the dirty work for him. Somebody out there, some anonymous entity—government, it usually turns out to be—is supposed to pick up our garbage, educate our children, look after our old folks, enforce the laws, and maintain national security. We are entitled to such services, and we expect them; indeed, some of us describe them as human rights. We will pay for the work—albeit grudgingly and not always generously—but we will not do it ourselves.

Our civic virtue is nearly exhausted by the act of tax-paying. For the rest, we depend upon bureaucratic mercenaries. How much law and order would there be in a modern national society if we relied upon all adults, acting out of their sense of duty as citizens, to serve as law-enforcement agents? I suspect that our reaction against the idea of the vigilante is not exclusively attributable to our abhorrence of the abuses that people who take the law in their own hands may commit, but owes something to our aversion to the idea of serving, ourselves, as amateur policemen. Many of our professional policemen would affirm that our sense of civic duty does not operate so strongly as to make us willing to give them assistance beyond that purchasable with our tax money. One of the many good reasons for having a professional police force is the fact that our sense of public duty does not impel us to act to uphold the law ourselves. Our attitude toward the national security function is not fundamentally different. Increasingly, we expect to be able to buy national defense, to hire our defenders. We rely, for security purposes, less on our civic virtue than on our affluence.

The trouble with the international system is that, unlike the state, it has found no substitute for civic virtue in the matter of law enforcement. Both balance of power and collective security propose do-it-yourself systems for enforcement of world order, thereby inspiring modern man to look desperately for someone else to do the job. Americans of past generations invested their hopes in international courts, proposing to let judges keep order in the world while they sat in the audience, basking in the knowledge that they had righteously promoted the rule of law in international relations. President Wilson offended them by contriving a League of Nations that was to rely heavily upon the United States to do the job; they had wanted to hire judges, and Wilson asked them instead to enlist as policemen. After World War II, many Americans supported the idea of world government, and I suspect that much of the appeal of that idea lay in its promise to contrive a Great Somebody who would deal with the problem of upholding world order. The theory of collective security, like that of balance of power, tells us that there is nobody here but just us states. The states that constitute the international system will keep order, or there will be none. The great virtue of collective security is its realistic facing up to this fundamentally important fact. Its great weakness is that it makes demands upon international civic virtue that cannot be met. Collective security demands that people do for the world what they may not be willing to do even for their own states. Neither the political elites nor the ordinary people who constitute the states of the world are prepared to accept the obligations of a collective security system.

NOTES

[1] Address by Wilson, June 7, 1918, in Ray S. Baker and William E. Dodd, eds., *The Public Papers of Woodrow Wilson: War and Peace* (New York: Harper, 1927), I, p. 227; Gilbert Murray, *From the League to U.N.* (London: Oxford University Press, 1948), p. 72.

[2] Murray, *op. cit.*, pp. 65, 72–73.

[3] Statement by Eugene V. Rostow to Committee I of the United Nations General Assembly, Oct. 21, 1981. U.S. Department of State, Current Policy Series No. 336, Nov. 1981.

[4] See, for instance: Kenneth W. Thompson, "Collective Security Re-examined," *American Political Science Review*, XLVII, No. 3 (Sept. 1953), pp. 753–772; Arnold Wolfers, *Discord and Collaboration* (Baltimore: Johns Hopkins, 1962), pp. 167–204; Inis L. Claude, Jr., *Power and International Relations* (New York: Random House, 1962), pp. 94–204.

[5] William H. Taft and William J. Bryan, *World Peace* (New York: George H. Doran, 1917; reprinted, 1973, by Jerome S. Ozer, Publishers).

[6] G. Lowes Dickinson, *Causes of International War* (London, 1920, 1928; reprinted, Garland Library of War and Peace, 1972), pp. 70, 74.

[7] *Ibid.*, pp. 34, 38–39, 40–41.

[8] *Ibid.*, p. 36.

[9] I have relied upon a transcript of this CBS "Face the Nation" program supplied by the United States International Communications Agency in Jerusalem, dated March 10, 1981.

[10] Murray, *op cit.*, pp. 99, 106–108, 123, 197.

[11] *Ibid.*, p. 40.

[12] *Ibid.*, pp. 75, 117.

[13] *Ibid.*, p. 74.

[14] *Ibid.*, pp. 38, 55, 68.

[15] Thomas O'Toole, "Draft Signup Grace Period is Extended," *The Washington Post*, Jan. 15, 1982, p. A-20.

DATE DUE

NOV 5 1987			
OCT 1 2 1994